For Two Beacons

Touching The Sky

Best thoughts for all
your skies

Banks of the Rain
20 October '01

Denise

Books by Denise Low

Dragon Kite
Quilting
Spring Geese
Starwater
Selective Amnesia
Vanishing Point
Tulip Elegies: An Alchemy of Writing

Edited by Denise Low

Kansas Poems of William Stafford
Confluence: Contemporary Kansas Poets
30 Kansas Poets

For Barbara
and Dennis,

Touching The Sky

Essays by

Denise Low

Flint Hills Photography by George Kren

PENTHE Publishing
P.O. Box 994
Lawrence, KS

Acknowledgements

An earlier version of "New Tenants" first appeared in Kestrel 1 (1993).

"Touching the Sky" first appeared in What Kansas Means to Me (Lawrence: University Press of Kansas, 1989).

"Quiltmaker" first appeared in the fine press edition Quilting (Holiseventh Press, 1983).

"Winter Solstice" first appeared in Kansas City Star 20: 11. Reprint in TIWA 2 (1993).

"Lightning" first appeared in Cottonwood 48 (1993).

"Agreements with Snakes" first appeared in Kiosk 8 (1992).

"Making Garden" first appeared in Well, Well, Well! (1994).

The author expresses gratitude to the many people who contributed to this work: Dorothy Bruner Dotson, William Francis Dotson, Thomas Weso, Jane Ciabattari, James Gilkeson, Carolyn Doty, Diane Willie, Sally McNall, Kelly Kindscher, Jim Hoy, Tom Averill, Carol Estes, Barnaby Ruhe, Stephen Meats, and Dalies Devine. The publisher also wishes to express his gratitude to Lois Greene, Margo Kren, Diane and Gary Tegtmeier, Bill and Laurie Ward, Mr. and Mrs. W. F. Dotson, Dalies Devine, Martin Olson, Deane White, and Kim Bergeson for their support of this project.

ISBN: 0-9632475-8-1

Library of Congress Catalog Number: 94-068503

PENTHE Publishing

P.O. Box 994

Lawrence, KS 66044

Printed in the United States of America

Contents

For
Thomas Francis Weso

For
the Flint Hills and all grasslands

Introduction

Born, raised, educated, and employed as a professor in Kansas, Denise Low has gone out of her way to learn of all the state's facets.

In *Touching The Sky* the reader will find that Low has a profound grasp of history immediately past, history further back, and pre-history. This book reminds me that not much seems to escape her notice. She has studied quilts; indigenous peoples; flowers and animals and trees and brush; farming; small town life; libraries; schools; fossils; arrow points; rivers large and small; the sky and its clouds; the turnpike and back roads; newspapers; the arts; cooking and recipes and canning; eagles, hawks, owls and seemingly all the other birds; and much, much more.

Working from the urgently held belief that everything that has ever happened in Kansas affects all that is happening and everything that ever comes to happen, she knows when the Ice Age was and precisely where the ice stopped. Denise Low believes that in order to earn the right to her feelings, knowledge, and opinions, she must not only be an expert tracker of the current grid that is Kansas, but be thoroughly acquainted with all she can find down through what's gone before as well.

Poet, writer, editor, critic, mother, daughter, lover, seer, and fast friend, Low deserves everything that's coming with the publication of this memorable and affirming book.

G. Barnes,
Literary Coordinator,
Utah Arts Council

Like Gretel Ehrlich, Annie Dillard, and Terry Tempest Williams, Denise Low writes of her childhood, family, and land and of how all are interwoven. Low takes us through spaces of the prairie, evocative rooms in her memory that hold fire, snakes, friends, prairie plants, and sky. She celebrates them in a direct, non-sentimental way. Her writing is both spare and rich, like the prairie itself. Particularly inspiring is her essay about the experience in the aftermath of the plowing of the previously untouched 80-acre Elkins Prairie.

Terry Evans,
artist, photographer,
Salina, Kansas,

Denise Low ends her title essay with the words: "Kansas is a zone . . . where only the best part of the human spirit walks, touching both earth and sky at once." These words also speak for Low's own work, so rich in descriptive (earth) and spiritual (sky) power.

Now, in her first prose collection, *Touching The Sky,* Low explores a range of interests—from hairweaving to firing the Flint Hills, to her grandmother and the Haskell Earthworks Medicine Wheel. For Kansans, and for anyone else interested in exploring the connections of environment, history, and the life of the imagination, *Touching The Sky* will act as both witness and guide.

At the beginning of "Coordinates of my Existence," Low writes, "I grew up oblivious to my own historic stratum." The statement is an honest accounting and a promise to make herself, and her readers, more aware. All along, Denise Low has been providing such awareness to readers of her poetry.

In *Touching The Sky,* her quiet, steady prose enriches and enhances what can live in the imagination, for Low's words, like her heart, are grounded in place, but soaring in spirit.

Thomas Fox Averill,
writer-in-residence,
Washburn University

Touching The Sky

I. Flint Hills Journey

> *Trees refuse to follow from Topeka.*
> *The car radio loses contact*
> *and mumbles fuzz to itself.*
>
> *The highway bisects a moonscape*
> *and you are alone.*
>
> *If you see a diesel truck*
> *it lumbers like a beast*
> *lost from another age*
> *like you.*
>
> *Two sounds rise from the gullies*
> *and repetitious hills out there—*
>
> > *in summer*
> > *wind and waves of cicada drone*
> >
> > *in winter*
> > *only yelps of wind.*

The movie the *Wizard of Oz* stereotypes the prairie lands. Daily life on Aunt Em's farm, though imbued with warm relationships, is black and white; the fascinating land of Oz is in color. The scenery of the high plains is reduced to drab, two-dimensional sky, and all that matters is the foreground—the barn and chickens and farmhouse. As I grew up in Kansas, I absorbed the lessons of the movies and magazines, and I assumed that my native land around me was ordinary. I wanted to trade plain elm trees for the palm trees of television's *77 Sunset Strip* or *Adventures in Paradise*.

Sometimes when I was young, my unfashionable midwestern kingdom amazed me nonetheless. I loved looking at the first ridge of the Flint Hills west of town. The intense blue sky came down to a band of haze and then shaded, imperceptibly, into the purple hills themselves. Later I learned the Flint Hills sit atop an ancient mountain range, the Nemahas.

The night sky of stars was a brilliant airscape. When I was ten, I wanted to become an astronomer to fully grasp their existence. Some intangible experience surrounded me that was as completely real as long afternoons of sun. Perhaps it was simply beauty: the grand scale of sky—a manifestation of infinity itself—evoked active appreciation.

But it took many years for me to trust my own aesthetics and to see the full spectrum of colors in the Kansas sunlight.

First, I had children of my own. The media-free years of their early childhood was a recollection of my own enthusiasms. A wasp nest is worth long scrutiny, and time stretched and curved to fit each day's discovery. Sand dredged from the river for a sandpile was a diary of the river's travels. Tiny bits of quartz and flint and sandstone glittered on our fingers. We learned all the properties of dry, damp, and molded wet sand. Our back yard provided daily adventures with mud, bugs, wildfowers, cats, and blue jays. Following toddlers on their daily treks is an initiation into the mysteries of any place.

My second epiphany came when I accompanied the children to the local natural history museum. After the third and fourth trips I was not drawn to the La Brea tarpit exhibit with saber-toothed tigers and grinning wolves, or to the colorful tropical panorama of life zones. The exhibit I re-examined was in a far corner of the basement floor, findings from the Kansas River that flows through the Lawrence downtown, two miles from my house: a mastodon skull and tusks, a Folsom point, a giant Ice Age beaver skull, and an extinct bison skull with enormous horns. The mineralized brown bones came to life. The Folsom point fit itself onto the end of an oak shaft. Outside, the landscape shimmered beneath midday sun. Puddlings of terminal moraines and escarpments of limestone ocean bottoms would never look the same. Encouraged by museum education programs, I began to learn the bioregion that includes Kansas. The past opened under my feet, where underlying sediments preserve thousands of years of species. When mere human measures of time are set aside, this land is as exotic as Neptune.

The top layer in northeastern Kansas, glacial drift deposits, is the southernmost boundary of four continental glaciers. The most extreme ice cover extended north of the Kansas River and east to the Blue River. The valleys in this area, now dotted with cornfields, once bulged with hundreds of feet of ice. In the north, the glacier was ten thousand feet thick, and it thinned as it reached its edge, Kansas, to two hundred feet. These spans require mental acrobatics to envision. But evidence is there. The ice carried tons of rock and silt. Pink quartzite boulders, relocated from Minnesota outcroppings, are now common yard ornaments. And these transients carry within them the mystery of the Precambrian Age, the oldest geologic time, when they were formed. The finer debris of retreating glaciers was loess, valuable topsoil that supports cattle and grain. Our morning cereal comes from crushed Ice Age rocks.

The habitat south of the ice sheet—most of Kansas—was pine forest then, sustained by cool, damp weather patterns. The climate was more temperate, and supported a variety of large-scale mammals.

These incredible *mega fauna* lived in today's pastures and suburbs, in a different section of time.

A cache of fossilized Ice Age bones washed into the Kansas River, perhaps during the 1951 flood, and spectacular finds on sandbars are possible. A college student found a mammoth skull, with curled tusks, buried in sand. My son Daniel found an extinct bison molar. Specimens of a forgotten bestiary abound underneath us, in a zoo fenced by stone.

There were herds of musk oxen and wild boars, mastodons, and huge bison two or three times the size of present day "buffalo." Giant sloths, as tall as houses, grazed on thorn trees. Terrible predators lived well: saber-toothed *smilodons* (several species), dire wolves, and most awesome, a cat-faced bear, *arctodus simus*. With a minor adjustment in time (mammoth remains only 6,000 years old have been found in Kentucky) the place called Kansas becomes more interesting than anywhere on Earth today. The Ice Age continues to exist in the journals of paleontologists like *The Mammoth Trumpet;* the collections of sandbar combers; and the minds of children growing up along the rivers. Maybe a tracing of those animals' spirits remains in the erratic, spinning particles that hover about these humid river valleys.

II. Mothers' Day Drive

We head north, toward Lawrence,
into limestone country.
Highway slices stone,
exposing multitudes of skeletons,
hills filled with fossils—
crinoids, corals, clams.

Calcite
like these thick bones of mine
first formed grain by grain
from my mother's bloodstream.

Seedling cottonwoods
push up through rock cracks.
Layers of old ocean debris
hold up this spring's grass.

Glacial drift, bluffs of loess, and sand dunes of south-central Kansas are only recent surface decorations. The real foundation of the heartland is solid masses remaining from ancient swamps and oceans. Seawater covered almost all of the central continent hundreds of millions of years ago, and during long cycles, the seas rose and fell many times. Organic life began in the seas, and even now its remains sustain us.

In Kansas the sequence of geologic ages begins in the oldest eastern rocks and continues west. Southeastern Kansas surface rocks are solidified masses of coal swamps, 330 million years old. West of them are the Osage Cuestas, strata formed by Pennsylvanian seas, filled with clams and other marine life. Next, the Flint Hills are a band left from the Permian ocean (250 million years old). Bedrock for the rest of the state is a Cretacean system—chalk—that preserves more developed marine reptiles and fish. A spewing of eroded soil from the Rocky Mountains lies over western Kansas, forming the expanses of level horizon, but underneath is this last sea of 63 million years ago.

A car trip across the state is 400 miles, but it also traces almost 300 million years from the Missouri border to Colorado. As elevation increases, rainfall declines; the damp gulf stream full of rainclouds has hastened the erosion of eastern Kansas, exposing older rock deposits, and this deepening valley uncovers even some Cambrian rocks further east into Missouri.

Fossil remains suggest dramas of survival and failure. A writer has daily reminders of survival and mortality in stones used for buildings, fences, and landscaping. The campus of Kansas State University is built of this "vernacular" limestone of eastern Kansas, and a nineteenth-century coffee shop where I like to write has rock walls filled with enigmatic fossil shells.

Pennsylvanian limestone includes corals, one-celled animals the size of wheat kernels (foraminifers), and many mollusks. These mussel-like animals appear to have dug into solid stone as a last hiding place. More unusual are the crinoids—sea animals that look like ferns. The segmented stems support a lily-like flower formed by tentacles. We can only wonder at the original coloring. Primitive sharks were marauders in the warm seas of this time, and a few last trilobites can be found here. These tiny crab ancestors flourished since early Cambrian times and died out gradually.

Also remarkable are fossils of the next period, the Cretaceous. Niobrara chalk in western Kansas holds in suspension many reptiles, large fish, and early birds. Swimming just below an apparently bland surface of wheatfields are mosasaurs—sea reptiles that resemble large snakes with fins. Another menace was the pleisiosaur, an alligator-like reptile. Many varieties of sharks developed to feed on clams, ammonites (related to today's nautilus), and sharp-toothed fishes. Humans would have no chance in this violent competition.

These forgotten animals, embedded in rock, provide mental sustenance for Kansans: they force the mind to reenvision the daily landscape; they testify to a dimension of time that carries each locale through remarkable transformations; they give perspective to individual life as well as the life cycle of an entire species. And the bones and shells of past ocean life soften, year by year, into topsoil that magically nourishes the present generation.

III. West

> *Here the sky gives clarity to each tree—*
> *a gray hand on the horizon,*
> *perpendicular on horizontal.*
>
> *The long slope of miles*
> *approaching the mountains,*
> *moving always into blue blue haze.*
>
> *Each tree a slow traveler on this road.*

Returning to the ground level and present time, a singular beauty unfolds on the prairies. The buttes and ridges do not have the drama of cities or mountains or ocean, but nothing interrupts the sweep of sky around the horizon or diminishes its activities. The confrontation between earth and sky is as intense as the coastlines where water meets earth. And the unbroken sky is a transparent, barely physical element that teases the senses as well as the imagination. Untouchable sunsets create concentrations of colors; the air itself is tinged plum or cerise or brass.

The earth's constant rotation creates prevailing winds that sculpt snow drifts into crusty ocean waves. In June the wind shakes spores from pine trees and fills air with cotton from female cottonwood trees. Dust storms, volcanic ash, dried leaves, and hawks are all visible travelers on unseen currents. Wind, focused in tornado funnels or disseminated by Caribbean Gulf breezes, constantly exerts its invisible pressure. Every creature on the plains learns the effects of winds that, like God, no one has ever seen.

Fog, mist, drizzle, rain, hail, and cloudbursts have immediate tactile dimensions, but the silent extremes of temperature do not. Snow blown by the northern winds is visible, but not the wind itself, nor the nightly tides of winter cold. Temperatures can reach forty degrees below zero (Lebanon, 1905). The searing heat of summer, up to 120 degrees, can

create a womb-like warmth. During a hot spell the temperature hardly dips below ninety degrees, so the air presses against skin like a mother. Greetings among people, the prosaic comments on weather, are attempts to give verbal texture to unseen elements working freely on the land. Those who do not read the sky attentively pay a price. The blizzards, windstorms, burning heat, and even lightning cause fatalities each season.

In a prairie town there is no seaward or mountainside direction. But with the land exposed on all sides, the sky's four directions reveal distinct characteristics. The seasonal calendar is associated with north for winter, south for mild summer weather, and west for the next day's weather. Space and time join together; the immediate future can be seen in clouds forming on the western edge of sky. Occasionally, time runs amok, and a storm blows yesterday's clouds back from the east. And of course the rising eastern sun, its rays uninterrupted, renews existence each day. No wonder Indian nations base their understanding of creation on the four sacred directions and the place each being has within the hoop of the horizon. This circle is most whole on the grasslands.

The Ghost Fort of Eureka

In small Kansas towns, history blows away quickly. Children grow up and move away to more prosperous parts of the country. Dust fills in the wheel ruts of the Oregon Trail and the Santa Fe Trail, or highway asphalt covers over old traces. Wood rots, and limestone walls fall into disrepair. In the small town of Eureka, Fort Montgomery has become like a ghost town. Its grounds—wooden stockade and a dozen buildings—once covered several acres, but they are nearly gone. Only a few walls remain, and people who could tell the fort's story rest under marble slabs in the cemetery.

One clear winter day I walk through the streets of Eureka, to First Street and Oak, where the only remaining vestige of Fort Montgomery is a shell of the old stable, built of vernacular limestone piled neatly around door beams and window frames. In recent times one wall has been reinforced as a support for an auto body shop. The rest of the building is empty, waiting to give in to the force of gravity, like the other buildings that preceded it into oblivion—the mess hall, the officers' quarters, the barracks. Yellow limestone squares are laid in such a regular pattern, that from a distance the rows give the appearance of a tightly woven rug.

Men working in the auto body shop this cold day have no notion of the history of the site, nor do the women on Main Street who go to shop at the antiques, or "collectibles," store. Pamphlets describing tours of Greenwood County do not mention the nearly invisible fort. Yet its presence changes the mood of the corner, just off Main Street, just away from the trickle of traffic in this small ranching town in the Flint Hills.

Like any town of size in this area, there is one repository of historic facts, and that is the Greenwood County Historical Society. It is housed in a storefront on North Main, and among its curiosities—an arrow in an animal vertebrae and a netting to protect a horse from flies—there is a pencil drawing of the old Fort Montgomery. It shows the Verdigris River at the top of the map, two coyotes, the stockade of wooden logs, and the square buildings. It resembles any fort erected by the U.S. Army during the 1860's, including the restoration at Fort Scott, Kansas. It seems, however, an anomalous object on the open prairieland of the Flint Hills. The only trees growing in the area now are scrub trees along the creeks and small rivers. In the 1860's the Osage and other Indians still fired the dry grass in spring or fall to keep the land open to herds of elk and buffalo. The lumber must have been hauled in, and in fact it was replaced by limestone from the hills themselves. Many buildings in Eureka still are built of stone. Cattle keep the foliage chewed to the ground, and trees are still scarce.

One drama enacted on these plains occured during the Civil War. In Oklahoma, fullboods of the Creek Nation conflicted with the mixed-blood faction over slavery. Brother fought brother over this issue, and the remaining group of fullblood Creeks fled north to Kansas, a free state refuge. Their goal was Ft. Montgomery. It was winter, and women and children traveled with the group. Continuous winds made the chill even more intense. Snow fell, and creeks were frozen over. Before they could reach Ft. Montgomery, their pro-slavery relatives caught up with them. Only a few survivors reached Ft. Montgomery.

This story is a few paragraphs in the Greenwood County history book. Those Creek Indians slaughtered on the way to Ft. Montgomery are almost forgotten. And the remains of the fort itself are barely discernible among the storefronts of a contemporary town. If I had not heard the story, I would never have guessed the stable wall to be anything but a pattern of stacked stones.

Mourning Wreaths of Human Hair

I have only seen hair wreaths in Kansas. This is not to say they do not exist elsewhere, since Victorian Kansas culture was second-hand East Coast, third-hand European, and some Native American. American adaptations to frontier life had already developed in Pennsylvania or Ohio or northern Missouri, so wreath-making, like quiltmaking, was brought west. Glenway Wescott, a nineteenth century writer, described a wreath made of hair in a Wisconsin novel. Still, mention of hair wreaths—or other mementos made of hair—is rare. They were everyday objects of popular culture, seldom noted in any way by writers or scholars of the time.

Hair tatting was a women's art form—undervalued and poignantly expressive. My grandmother, Carrie Strittmatter Dotson, wrote about a sense of unfulfilled yearning after a lifetime on the Kansas plains, "I have always felt in myself a quest for something. Certain chords of music bring this feeling, a sort of nostalgia for something—what?" She wrote poetry as well as she could, conscious that she lacked education, and sang in the church choir. This same impulse drove women who made rags into quilts, and also women who used strands of hair in needlework. They kept jars on their dresser drawers to collect hair from their brushes. From this free thread they made lace. They alchemized the ordinary into objects of beauty.

Antique dealers do not often sell hair ornaments of any kind, since they are not showy collectibles. They are small and made of bristly human hair, not amber or silver. Most often they stayed in private collections, with the original families and their descendants. Hair becomes brittle and breaks apart. And such ornaments are often of limited historical use, since they are difficult to trace. Our family has a civil-war era photograph album filled with nameless men and women and children who are my ancestors. My great-great grandparents felt no sense of their future generations who would want dates and explanations. Their sense of history was immediate. In the same way, plaited strands of hair had great meaning to families at the time, but once names are lost, hair is as anonymous as faces—and impossible to identify.

To people of the 1800's, locks of hair, like photographs, were important—and still individual—keepsakes. Loved ones could be remembered through this real part of their whole body. Few people could afford painted portraits, and they paid professional photographers for formal sittings just a few times in their lives, but hair could be clipped any time. For poor migrants to the western prairies, the cherished lock of hair was sometimes the only remembrance of someone left in the old country. This could be the only continuity with their past.

Sometimes women preserved collections of hair clippings in pages of copy books, much like photograph albums. In *The Grandmothers*, Wescott described "a copy book bound in vermilion paper with two or three tiny garlands of hair on each foxed but substantial page." This collection of fifty-six locks included many variations, "...braided hoops, medallions like bits of Spanish lace, and spider webs, combinations of loops and zigzags and coils and shadowy scallops." Sometimes women simply tied a curl with a ribbon and kept it in an envelope or in pages of the Bible. But more elaborate collections showed the ingenuity of artisans accustomed to needlework from the age of three.

The Douglas County museum in Lawrence, Kansas has a rare album of hair snippets. Descendants knew the family history, and it represents the story of typical settlers in this area. Emma Ely was born in Pennsylvania and married Joseph Miller in 1863. The couple moved to a Kansas farm in 1878 and lived there until 1911, when they moved to town, to Lawrence, Kansas. She died in 1921 at the age of eighty. The album has a cross-stitched cover dated May 8, 1858, so she began the collection of hair when she was a girl of seventeen. She carried it with her on the trip to Kansas and continued adding to it as a young bride. Emma Ely Miller did list the names with each curl or length of hair stitchery, and sometimes she added a poem, but she dated nothing. And she felt no need to explain obvious relationships of siblings and friends to future readers—to us.

Like Kentucky death quilts, hair tokens can have the added dimension of a memorial. When a family member died suddenly, hair could be saved as a last earthly bond. The smallest lock in Emma Miller's album was from her stillborn son. The short poem with it reads,

The cares of heart never knew
Never felt the blight of sin
The pearly gates have let me through
Right angels led me in.

Today I find the language awkward, but these words express grief of a mother far from her own parents. She found comfort in poetry and the fragile strands. Fanny Appleton Longfellow, wife of Henry Wadsworth Longfellow, lost her child Mary. Before the funeral, she wrote in her diary that she "cut a few locks from her holy head." Years later, ironically, her own death was caused by fire as she was sealing curls into envelopes with wax.

Simple locks of hair, also worn in lockets, could be made into objects of practical use. In one family a deceased mother's hair was braided into a watch fob. Her sister presented it to the surviving son as a daily reminder of his mother.

Perhaps these practices seem macabre now, but at the time, and until the middle of the twentieth century, people saw death more often. Many children died, grandparents died, and women died in childbirth. Grief was a part of life, and there was a need for its expression.

On the prairie, the Lakota people had a parallel practice of saving a lock of hair from a person who died. This was part of a religious ceremony called Keeping the Soul. Black Elk describes purification of the hair with sweet grass smoke. Then, after prayers, "The lock of hair was wrapped in sacred buckskin, and this bundle was placed at a special

29

place in the tipi." For the year of mourning, the bundle was cared for carefully, until the Releasing of the Soul ceremony, and then the hair could be "kept by the family, if they wished, as something of a remembrance." Joseph Epes Brown explains that the hair became a focus for the soul, "intermediate between the gross body and the pure spirit." This allowed for an extension of the soul's individual state, and so it could be purified by prayers and ceremonies.

European American immigrants did not have the same religious rites, but no doubt prayers accompanied work during months that women spent crocheting their memorials to the departed.

Funeral wreaths were the most elaborate form of hair crafting. These were the size of Christmas wreaths today, and in each household they would hang in the parlor. Women wrapped wire frames with hair from all family members who had passed on. Over this foundation they would add lacework. Wescott describes a wreath with intricacies of "Turks'-cap lilies, frayed leaves, and swollen buds."

Everyone would recognize the family members by the shades of color, and wreaths became heirlooms that tied together two or three generations of the living and the dead. Hair wreaths have distant relationship to classical Greek and Roman leaf wreaths—the laurels of victors and myrtle wreaths worn by party goers to maintain sobriety—but on isolated farms, wreaths were never meant to be worn. Coiled and knotted hair told stories of sorrow, not celebration.

*

I first saw a funeral wreath of human hair when I was a child at the local historical society. It was jumbled among other relics—a skull with an arrowhead in it, a Victrola that played wax rolls, doll houses—all shown by a frizzled old man who seemed antique himself. All of the group of children stood amazed at the skull. The man then showed us buttontop shoes, lace bloomers, ceramic knick-knacks, and a wreath, offhandedly saying it was made of hair. He took time to explain it was a mourning wreath, made from hair of family members who had died.

The hair fibers still glistened that afternoon, a hundred years later. I was about twelve, and I had not seen a dead person before. The sight of the skull and the hair wreath at once—there in the basement of the bank building—scared me. The dark hallway was no comfort, nor the brass walls of the elevator as I fled back into daylight.

Years later I saw a second wreath in the Chase County Historical Museum, in an overlooked corner. The curled designs still retained an essence of another history, preserved like dried herbs left from the summer garden. Most of people's remains return to earth, but strands of hair can still join together metal frame, tatted lilies and the gaze of the beholder. The ornament presents an odd intimacy with long-dead strangers.

The one I saw was from a family of brunettes, with just one medallion of gray hair and one scroll of a child's fine hair, sandy blond. At first it appeared to be a muff or collar made of lacey fur—something animal, not human. The floral design had no true flowers, but rather shapes evolved from tatting stitches, constructed in patterns parallel to nature's forms. Deep chestnut fibers formed rosettes and Josephine knots, twisted around wire and springs, with one spring worn bare. Outside the door the Cottonwood River flowed east, and the Flint Hills stretched every direction around the room. In my hands brown hair formed intricate designs, twisting time into its own dimension.

I know the mourning wreath is still there now, in that old room of dark wood and dust, outlasting all names and all griefs.

Quiltmaker

Great-grandmother Dotson,
sodhouse settler I met once
and never forgot—

> *"A daughter of the late Isaiah and Harriet Sinks Scott*
> *Born January 17, 1869 at Dayton, Ohio."*

> *"Stricken dead after visiting all evening with friends"*
> *Newton, Kansas, 1954.*

This rainy afternoon
I open her quilts on my wedding bed—

> *Flower Garden, rosettes of white and green*
> *Wedding Ring, locking circles of pink*
> *Grandma's Fan, plumes of blue and red.*

I remember the taste of cream pie.

I remember her diary—

> *"rain since Monday"*
> *"I suffer today from rose fever."*
> *"Today we have a healthy girl baby."*

I look in the dresser mirror—

> *her brown eyes*
> *her quilts spread behind me.*

"Quiltmaker" recalls one of my earliest memories: car trip to Newton, Kansas, to visit my great-grandmother. Even as a small child I was awed by the reverence my parents had for her. I remember sitting on her lap and feeling the strength of her personality. As a high school student I came across her diary—a simple, moving testimony of daily affairs—and even later, after my marriage, I received several quilts she had made with friends. A final impetus for the poem was the discovery of her obituary, carefully preserved by my grandmother.

Having inherited these fabric assemblages of my great-grandmother's daily history, I was reluctant to use them. I found myself caught between wanting to cover myself with their rich patterns, and wanting to preserve them, crisp and unfrayed, for my own grandchildren.

Quiltmaking is an apt metaphor for the making of art. The poetry I like best, in fact, is a synthesis of everyday objects and events, chosen from a rag-bag stockpile and transformed by the human touch. My friendships, too, parallel a piecing process, where shared experiences are pulled together into new patterns. The metaphor works on many more levels. Beyond artifice, quilts themselves are optically interesting, their designs foreshadowing modern taste, yet retaining tradition.

I myself do not quilt, or even sew. Nonetheless, I feel included in the vast circle of women who have had families and have tried to make objects of utility and beauty from fabric or yarn. A friend tells me of settling into a hand-knit sweater one winter day, pulling an afghan over his legs, and becoming aware of the presence of the knitters. Such nurturance is an inheritance threaded through the generations.

Carrie Adel Strittmatter Dotson, 1885-1980

In her journals my grandmother copied Chinese poems. I think of her in Newton, Kansas, during the 1920's reading Tu Fu, Li Po, and Yuan Mei between women's club meetings and choir practice. She knew the British canon of poetry from school, as well as Longfellow and James Whitcomb Riley. Those days grade school children memorized rhymes starting with kindergarten. But in that small town, remote on the flat croplands, the T'Ang dynasty poets spoke to her most intimately. She always had the deepest feelings for the Chinese poets, perhaps because they, too, lived in a landscape of endless sky. She saw that sky in reproductions of Chinese paintings.

There was no other reason for my grandmother's attraction to Asian arts in the small town—just west of the Midwest proper, on the route of the cattle drives from Texas to Wichita or Abilene. Even into the 1960's cattle wintered in Texas and came north on the railroad to fatten on spring grasses. She followed that same route in 1914 when her groom brought her north to live among Yankees. She was raised in San Antonio, and though she responded to the Kansas landscape with poetry and water colors, she had no firsthand experience of country life.

Her favorite poem was a long elegy by a Chinese father who had lost a five-year-old girl. She read the ten pages over and over to herself, and she told me it was the most beautiful verse ever written:

A friend comes with hurried steps
To tell me
That the old neighbors have arrived
To take the child away.
All try to persuade me to take the matter calmly—
But from their own eyes come torrents of salt tears.

Two days ago
There came a heavy fall of snow,
And the pools and ponds were covered with thick ice.
Playing, I tied some bits together,
To make an imitation of a bell.
I called you to strike it—
"Lang, lang, lang."
Today the ice still lies upon the ground,
But your little body is gone forevermore. . . .

As a youngster, I did not understand how any poem about death could be beautiful, but I reread it years later, and it was indeed as poignant as an autumn chrysanthemum.

Grandmother Carrie loved chrysanthemums, the last flowers of the season, because they bloomed at her birthday in November. She told me they were symbols to the Chinese artists, as were plum blossoms and pines and bamboo. Plum blossoms evoked the spirit of spring, and pine represented old age. Bamboo showed strength through its flexibility. Each Chinese ink painting or poem told stories of human passions with flowers and trees.

Outsiders call Kansas flyover country, and perhaps the small towns are drab to some people. But my grandmother made beauty in her home. She collected cloisonne vases and a *Kuan Yin* of translucent soapstone. She sang in the Methodist church choir, and she read Chinese poetry to her grandchildren.

*

Carrie Dotson left only two original journals of prose: a family history, and, in a dimestore autograph book given to me at Christmas of 1958, she wrote scenes from her own childhood in San Antonio. In other notebooks she also wrote poetry, and she left enough poems for a small volume published after her death.

But most of the journals she left were full of quotations from books and the Bible. Her own voice is diluted by them, and I wonder at her selflessness. Was she deferring to voices of authority, by copying famous people's words? Was she honoring them? My mother later told me Grandmother Carrie grew up very poor and had no chance for a higher education. I am not sure she even graduated from high school. She always expressed respect for educated people, and reading was her self education. She reread *Anna Karenina* every year, and she had read the entire Bible many times. I have wondered about her love of the tragic Russian novel, a contrast to her conventional marriage. The story of Anna's failed love resembles the tragedies of many operas, another of her loves, and perhaps this was an outlet for her romanticism. She lived in a small town where even flirtations were scandalous.

In the front of the short family history, also written in 1958, she inscribed the book with quotations from eighteen diverse authors. They included Lillian Hellman, Emily Dickinson, Shakespeare, Ralph Emerson, James Thompson, Hippocrates, Virginia Scott Miner, David Grayson, William Wordsworth, S. Browne, Don Marquis, George Bernard Shaw, the Talmud, Eric Goffe, and George Burchard. The excerpts were all carefully chosen to reflect her theme of ancestors, and she consciously referred to one, the Burchard quotation about reincarnation, as a statement of her own thoughts about mortality, "Maybe when you read *The Lost Continent of Mu* on the front pages of this book you can account for my feelings." She turned to this eccentric author to express the most personal beliefs. She never talked about these ideas in conversation except once, when she told me she thought the afterlife occurred on other stars.

Perhaps Grandmother Carrie's reference to the great writers was not a passive acceptance of the authority of educated men and a few women. Perhaps it was a continuation of the pattern of her education—rote memorization. She describes this, "When we were little we'd have to recite pieces, as we called them, we started with four liners and as

37

we grew we had longer pieces. The four liners consisted of such—"Here I stand on two little chips/ Please come kiss my sweet little lips." She describes the "four liners" and finally the dramatic presentation of ghost stories like "Old Tompie Is Dead." From her earliest times, she was given verses to memorize line by line, and perhaps the painstaking copying of quotations parallels the way she learned poems by heart.

Implicitly, along with verses, Grandmother Carrie's parents and older siblings taught her to value words for not only their wisdom, but also entertainment value. She describes family evenings of homemade dramas and songs. Her greatest regret about becoming old was the loss of her singing voice. The writings in her journals date after that time, when she no longer had that means of expression.

My grandmother also used her address book, inscribed with quotations, and her diaries as collages of her daily life. They served as scrap books, and she filled them with clippings, stickers, and cut-up photographs as well as gift inserts and small broadsides of poems she had self published. When I began to keep journals, I decided to bring everything together in one notebook, so I too could have a place of continuity. I still do this, and I wonder how much my own mode of journal-keeping reflects my grandmother's approach.

*

When Grandmother Carrie died in 1980 I was the only grandchild, out of seven, left in Kansas. I inherited her *Kuan Yin* statues, a Bible from 1912, and diaries. In her writings she passed on more than some children's stories and family histories. She also gave me a pattern for how to engage with the world. Through her I understood that wise words of famous people could be copied over in my own hand, and made my own. I learned that words were worth saving, along with perfumed handkerchiefs, silk fans, and rosebuds. And along the way I learned that I had an identity that I could express freely on the written page.

I kept my own first diaries, small volumes from Woolworths, starting in fourth grade. A favorite Christmas gift then was a new diary, the kind with a lock and key clasp. Like Samuel Pepys, I worked out elaborate systems of codes so my sister could not find out what boys I liked and other important information. Like my grandmother, I put colored bird stickers in it to make it beautiful, especially since my penmanship was poor. By junior high I had a small spiral bound notebook in which I started to record poems and thoughts. After college, and after my two sons were in grade school, I started to keep regular journals, and at first they, too were a catalogue of books I had read, like the pages of quotations I saw written in my grandmother's green-ink cursive. I never had her sense of melody, so pen and paper have been my voice for many years. Perhaps my inheritance is the music of language, in the written and spoken conversations that link together one generation to the next. T'Ang dynasty poetry, with its mystical clarity, was my first model for writing. I experienced my first taste of these mountain poets with my grandmother Carrie, from the flat fields of central Kansas.

Coordinates of My Existence

In Lawrence, two-hundred-million-year-old lime stone underlies the soil, a buff-colored stone composed of sea fossils. These calcite stones are the underground scaffolding of the country, and above ground they appear in fences, at roadcuts, and even in downtown buildings, where vernacular limestone was in use for decades. The past literally surrounds every living moment. So on the larger scale, details of my existence are especially random. Many coincidences contribute to my personal geography. The fact I am not a mussel or trilobite at this location is a variable of time. Nor am I a musk ox or giant beaver from the Ice Age period, though remains of these animals have been found in the Kaw River across town from Haskell Indian Nations University, where I teach. Mineralized bones of mastodons, dire wolves, peccaries, and giant bison also can be found in sandbars of the river.

I grew up almost oblivious to my own historic stratum. No one around me thought about the geology of the region except for Kansas History in seventh grade. Then I learned that good topsoil accounts for the wheat fields and soybean fields around Kansas towns. I did not yet learn this topsoil is recent, blown in after the Ice Age when the climate turned warm. Red patches of dirt in vacant lots came from Oklahoma, but mostly the ground was a deep black color, and I played for hours in black dust when I was a child. Playing with plastic cars, cows, and toy soldiers, under a great elm tree, are among my best memories.

I was born at mid-century, just six decades after the Wounded Knee massacre took place in South Dakota, two states north. As an adult I learned my great-great grandparents came West in the 1870's, after the Civil War, to homestead government land.

In 1862, the government granted any family 160 acres if they farmed it for five years, and the rainy years of the 1870's coincided with two of my ancestral grandparents' move to the prairielands of central Kansas. They left few family stories about their past or about the early days in Kansas. My father pieced together something of a chronology, but not much. He found some sermons his great-grandfather wrote when he lived in the backwoods of Kentucky. Besides the sermons, nothing remains of that past, before the Kansas migration, except a family Bible.

My direct forebears quickly left the land, moving from farms to towns in one generation. One great-grandfather was allergic to horses and moved to Kansas City as soon as he was able to leave home.

As I grew up in the 1950's and 1960's, the direct connection to my place of birth was vague. My family worried that I behave properly and do well in school. The landscape and its history were a backdrop that did not seem to matter that much in my pragmatic culture. My religion, Congregationalism, was set in an almost imaginary "Holy Land" across

the sea. Bible stories were a more serious set of fairy tales I learned and took on faith. There was no tangible reality to them besides the steepled church on the corner of State Street. I did love that building, and the vacant lot in back where we played baseball and touch football. I loved some of the older people.

My parents talked about their histories only later as they aged and began to reflect on their own place in the procession of generations. Because I was the only child left in Kansas, I heard these stories.

My surname came from a man who lived in Kansas only two years. My great-great grandfather William A. Dotson was dying of tuberculosis when he moved to Kansas in 1877, and he died in 1879. In the woods of Kentucky, where he preached Methodism and abolition, he might have contracted the disease. Or he could have become infected during the Civil War, when he served the Union as a chaplain for a Negro regiment. He wrote regular columns for the *Methodist Monthly,* and he relates his move to Pueblo, Colorado, for reasons of health.

But he could have emigrated from Kentucky because of the conflict within the church. During the war, the Methodist Church split over the issue of slavery, into two factions, the Methodist Episcopal Church South and North. In the border state of Kentucky, neighbors became enemies, and many Dotsons, or Dodsons, fought for the southern cause. I grew up with a relic of the Civil War: in an upstairs closet my father kept a flintlock rifle from that distant tragedy. He later gave it to a friend, and I am relieved to not have the burden of that heirloom.

I feel lucky to be able to trace William A. and his wife Martha Yewell Lashbrook as far back as their births, in 1834. The name Dotson apparently was English, a dialectic variation of Daudson, or David's son. But further research proves how abstract our parentage becomes. This obscure clan of Kansas Dotsons includes intermarriage with dozens of families—Strittmatter, Chapman, Lyon, Hulett, Foreman, Cummins, White, Burkhead, Hutchins and Ethelridge. Genealogy pushes the capacity of the mind very quickly: descendants of Charles and Ann Dodson of Virginia fill a two-thousand page book set. This lineage becomes a fishline tangle of snarls. I once heard a poet say that if you count fifty-two generations back, everybody is related to everybody.

In the early 1800's the U.S. government issued a hundred land grants to Dodsons in Kentucky alone. Perhaps one of the Williams listed in the Pulaski County records from 1803 was William A.'s father. The place name, Pulaski, is the most concrete evidence for relationship, as this was the birthplace of William A. Dotson. In later years he told the family that his parents, brother, and sister were all dead. As an orphan, he was raised in the Pulaski County household of Elizabeth Dotson Cummins and John Cummins. Though his father's name is not known for certain, his birthplace, Leitchfield, Kentucky, and the date, July 28, 1834, are the coordinates of his existence. He left dozens of written sermons, but little personal information.

I wonder at the multitude of histories that caused relatives to veer west instead of south or north, that caused my birthplace to be in Kansas.

The final coincidence occurred when my mother's family migrated to central Kansas. Grandmother Evelyn Miller Bruner moved from Kansas City to the flat plains, then covered with turkey-foot bluestem, where her husband found a job with the Santa Fe railroad. But a tornado struck the first night after she arrived. She packed up her bags the next morning and refused to live in that town. That storm caused her family to relocate, eventually, to another small town, Newton, where the William A. Dotson family resided. The family travels were complete, then, and my parents could attend school together, marry, and have four children—midcontinent and midcentury.

I live in Kansas, then, because of a tornado and because of a distant grandfather's tuberculosis. I used to be slightly embarrassed by my state and by the hard rrr's that punctuate my speech. But now I think of the locale as rare. There are barely two million people in a state that measures four hundred miles by two hundred miles. This is not a common location.

I step on topsoil that floats atop limestone bedrock. I work every day at Haskell, near wetlands of the Wakarusa River. Dozens of bird species live in the marsh, and skunks burrow under our buildings. I am here because of vagaries of weather and ancestors, and because I attended college in Lawrence. I loved this hilly river town when I came here in 1967, and I have never lived far away from it since then.

I was in this particular place in history when a teaching position opened up. So my fortunes joined with those of a hundred-year-old school run by the Bureau of Indian Affairs. At the time I knew nothing of the assimilation policies of the BIA boarding schools—nothing of the beatings of students who spoke their native language, or the certificates given to students who married whites. I had taught at the University of Kansas, and I liked contemporary Native American writers like James Welch and Leslie Silko. I liked the view of ridges beyond the Wakarusa River.

Denise Low

Ten years later I find myself on a campus that looks south over the Wakarusa Valley. The negative image of an Ice Age glacier can be seen in the carved-out terrain. The giant ice form has melted, but the valleys shows its contours. On campus I am amidst fields and old buildings with important history for many Indian families. I pass days in an old electronics building, Ross Hall, named after the Cherokee leader John Ross. When I enter a classroom, thousands of people's lives intertwine, if I count all the invisible ancestors who brought us to this moment. We hover among epochs as we walk through the halls and outdoors to the Wakarusa floodplain around us.

Agreements With Snakes

Most of the houses in my neighborhood marked the back property boundaries with fences, but snakes and kids ignored them. Even pedestrian dogs, unable to climb or slither, squeezed through slats and roamed at will. I always sensed snakes were out there within the flux of birds, squirrels, and cats, but I never saw any. This was an unstated agreement between me and them, like my similar arrangement with ghosts. Snakes were to use the yard at different times from me, probably at night, and I just would not see them. The same went for ghosts.

For me snakes were part of night, that profound eclipse of day, in this small town miles from Kansas City or Wichita. A few street lights did not illuminate much of the inky blackness, nor did the sprinkling of Milky Way. So I did not venture into the black void of night.

Once, after dark, my big brother reported a garter snake right by the garbage cans at the side door, so I knew snakes were nearby. I had no doubt many generations of garter snakes, racers, black snakes, and worse lived in our yard, a few feet away from my kitchen table, undisturbed by our human clatter.

Some snakes are active by day and others by night. In high school our biology teacher said each acre of the Flint Hills is home to seven copperheads. Garter snakes and grass snakes abound. But as much as I was outdoors during the day, I never saw snakes in our neighborhood.

Once a man came to clean out an old cistern three doors down, and neighborhood kids spotted him at this task. Over many years the plastered brick well had filled with silt and leaves. The handy man, dressed for a dirty job, performed various actions with shovels and other tools. As he worked he told us about seeing snakes in wells all the time, usually black snakes. Black snakes were feisty in the spring during courting season, he said, and he had been bitten often. And survived. I assumed all snakes were somewhat poisonous, and I could not imagine surviving any kind of bite. Thereafter, that old well had an aura of danger, and I stayed away from it. I knew mysterious reptiles continued to crawl into that well and under flinty places I could not see, just beyond my peripheral vision. Who knew how many snakes were at the bottom of that old well? What other secrets were hidden in muddy depths?

I do not know when I learned a fear of snakes. When I visited my uncle in Tennessee, he told me terrible tall tales of severed rattlesnake heads killing people. But my own family was more at peace with the snake kingdom. My father once brought me a tiny ring-necked snake for a pet. He had found it on a sidewalk in Wellington, Kansas, and brought it home for me. It was matte black, with a bright orange neck ring. The snake was the size of a pencil, and nimble among my fingers. I tried hard to communicate with it and feed it rolled peas of hamburger. I put grass in its box, but it went into a sluggish state. After a few days I put the comatose reptile under a stone in my mother's garden. The next spring I turned over the stone, expecting to find a skeleton of thin ribs and vertebrae. Nothing was there, so it must have crawled away to another incarnation.

My first encounter with a snake in its own territory was when I was fishing. I frequented a small lake, a diversion of the Neosho River contained by an earthen dam. Sunfish, largish bass, and snapping turtles filled the green water. One morning, before summer sun reached its sulfuric zenith, I was in a neck of the lake I usually avoided. Huge willow trees bent into the water, their strands of twigs forming lace curtains. I glanced through willow leaves into the shallows, and on a muddy bit of bank I suddenly made out a brown snake sunning itself. It was motionless, and it blended into the wet shoreline. I stood up. At a safe distance I could see the tell-tale triangular head and the sun glistening on a multitude of scales, just as it did on infinite small ripples of the brown water. I stared at the same spot, but without my seeing, the copperhead disappeared. One moment it was there. The next moment I saw only mud and silent water.

Diane Willie, a friend of Laguna Pueblo and Navajo heritage, tells me about growing up with snakes in New Mexico, and different attitudes about snakes from her father's people and her mother's people. Pueblo groups have lived in the Southwest for hundreds of generations, and their homes have been built within rocky cliffs, prime housing for snakes as well. After all this time, snakes have become family, with ancient stories and ceremonies like the Hopi dances with rattlesnakes. But Navajos, Athabascan newcomers to the area, traditionally live in more open places. Willie's Navajo grandmother had a more pragmatic approach to neighbors who happened to be snakes. She used the medicines of each species. She cured a son of snake bite by milking venom from another rattlesnake and using the liquid, mixed with herbs, as a poultice. All ceremonies with snakes were conducted with blessed—and also poison-milked—snakes.

Diane Willie grew up with her Navajo grandmother, who lived in a rocky canyon, and the children were warned to leave the snakes alone, especially rattlesnakes. The three sisters did not need to be frightened, just careful. And they were not to watch snakes courting or mating, for fear this would mark their own reproductive cycles.

The youngsters played together in a brushy ravine, building houses of stacked rocks and dirt. A rattlesnake happened to live next to the playhouse, so they terraced an earthen porch and pathway to her lair. This eased entry over sharp rocks for the reptile. The children understood the snake as a different kind of playmate, who also needed a cozy home.

For several years, the snake lived near the children's play yard. She followed them in their play, at a distance, and even seemed possessive. When the family dog came, she rattled and scared it away, then settled down. The snake continued to use the dirt pathway into her home among roots of an old tree. Although the snake was part of their daily lives, the sisters never named it like Anglo people would name a pet. She was Snake, who lived under the tree.

Once when the girls were out playing in the ravine, a rabid dog came into the neighborhood. Their uncle heard it coming and got his gun. The girls were unaware of the danger, busy as usual in their playhouse, with Snake nearby.

The crazed dog attacked. Snarling, he charged the sisters. They tried to run, but stumbled on rocks.

At this point the rattlesnake circled in front of the girls and sprang at the dog. She bit the dog several times, until it weakened and the uncle came to end the dog's misery. The snake never retreated. Willie says that was why they always thought Snake was a female, because of her protective nature.

In all her years in New Mexico, Willie never felt in danger from snakes. One summer she worked for the Forestry Service in northeastern Kansas, on the Kickapoo and Potawatomi reservations. She encountered garter snakes, bull snakes, blue racers, and a few timber rattlers. One morning she came upon dozens of blue racers swarming out of a rocky overhang and left the horde to their privacy. Another time a blue racer went through its spectacular defensive display, rushing at her and withdrawing, rustling the grass ferociously until Willie left its territorial boundary.

These midwestern snakes seemed more skittish—quicker to retreat or attack—than snakes in the Southwest. There are fewer shelters for them. Rocky exposures are rare, and many snakes have to share them, rather than spreading across miles of canyons and mountains. And perhaps they are conditioned to the reflexive fear of Anglo Midwesterners. Generations of Europeans have read Genesis and Cleopatra stories. A strong imprint of fear remains in the language, and also perhaps in more subtle expectations.

I now have a largish yard, with rocks and brush piles and many leafy plants. I dream about snakes three or four times a year, dreams I never understand beyond a feeling of their potential power. When we first moved in, I had the distinct feeling that snakes lived in my yard and wrote about them, in "Snakes,"

> They pass busy nights—
>   slipping wordless past sleeping dogs,
>   stalking toads in the garden.
>   Toward dawn
>   they circle the back porch.

I avoided going out alone after dark, when not only snakes, but also slugs, possums, badgers, and owls populate the world. Even behind car headlights, an opossum—with snout and beady eyes aglow—proves that creatures stranger than fiction exist. I agreed with myself that the back yard belonged to other beings after nightfall.

One summer morning, barefoot, I carried kitchen scraps to the compost heap. White butterflies circled broccoli plants in the garden. Midstep I saw a trian-gular brown head rise amongst day lily leaves, two yards in front of me. It had the mottled brown body of a copperhead. And the triangular head.

Midcoil, the snake saw an oncoming giant with pink feet.

We paused in a quick moment of mutual recognition, we two midwesterners, and then each of us retreated, with just the slightest veneer of dignity. I have not seen it since. But now, years later, I hope it is still near my back door.

New Tenants

I.

In 1991, eighty acres of untouched prairie, the Elkins Prairie, were plowed in Douglas County, my home county. This was not the Amazon rain forest, thousands of miles away, and this was not done by nineteenth-century buffalo hunters. A private landowner exercised his legal right to destroy, despite offers from the city to purchase this land. Protests meant nothing to him. The man was a developer from Kansas City, and he ordered the plowing at 3:00 a.m., to avoid legal and political action.

About ninety-five percent of the grasslands that once covered this country are now cultivated. Contrary to the popular image of prairies as wastelands of grass, they include hundreds of plant species besides the grasses. They cannot be easily restored, since prairie plants are exquisitely tuned to season and place. Spring flowering phlox and star grass develop and bloom within inches of autumn asters.

Shallow rooted plants alternate with deep-rooted ones, some grasses reaching twenty feet deep. Once plowed, the root systems—and balance—are forever destroyed. More aggressive plants like thistle invade broken prairie and choke out fringed orchids, butterfly plants, compass plants, milkweed, and many other edible and medicinal plants.

With friends I stole a frozen clod from the freshly plowed furrows of Elkins Prairie, hauled it to my garden, and waited for the long days of spring. I transplanted the one shaving of acreage into my back yard, a sunny opening beneath sycamores and oaks. Now the ancient dirt was within a city, surrounded by lawns and houses and a redwood fence. It was displaced like the old farmhouse down the block, a three-story frame house surrounded by flat ranch houses.

Six months later I identified twelve species in the chunk of dirt—a mushroom, four grasses, wildflowers, and more unknown seedlings. This small mite of dirt—so small I can reach my arms around it—is a microcosm of the eighty acres of virgin prairie it came from.

Of the two hundred species of plants in Douglas County prairie lands, these took up residence in my yard:

Stiff Goldenrod, *Solidago rigida*

An extension ladder, it generates new leaves at the tip, then another set of fuzzed leaves, and another. It grows from rhizomes, creating a colony from one root, one leaf repeated in a ring of plants. On the open prairie this wildflower root can spread out eight feet.

In my two-foot square of sod this first season, I find four plants of stiff goldenrod: one, the largest, builds a bloom stalk all summer, rung by rung; two young plants send up gray-green, rabbity-eared leaves; and in August after watering, fingerling shoots emerge.

In September the largest plant finally blooms at its tip, a flurry of flowerlets. The season's architecture comes to completion as sunlight glitters from within the petals.

Blue Aster, *Aster azureus*

The aster is solitary here, one of the largest plants after the long growing season. It blooms latest, after summer drought and autumn rains.

Stems are prominent, like bones. All summer the plant is a green skeleton covered by thin bits of foliage. The lancelot leaves find space in the grass around them, securing slivers of sunlight for their own.

Rough-skinned and stringy, isolated from its mates, the aster looks weedy until it explodes into hundreds of lavender stars.

The blooms, too, are tough, lasting even when sparkling frost covers the leaves.

Big Bluestem, *Andropogon errerdi*
Little Bluestem, *Andropogon scoparius*

Each clump of bluestem is the edge of the world. Far away, it blurs together to form a zone of haze and verdure, green at the base but turning bluish by gradations as sky mingles with plant matter. Millions of bluestem plants form this lapping edge, and the ultimate expanse of sky is purest blue, swept clean by wind.

At ground level another transformation occurs, unseen. Stems clench miles of twisted roots—labyrinths where decayed rocks and water turn into a fabric of sustenance. We walk over summer grass blind to this dimension of chemistry. Sometimes I can sense a wild energy, beneath me, or maybe I imagine it.

Fragrance is another unseen dimension that colors the winds. People breathe the grassy scent that arises in western distance.

My grandfather used to run many miles through Kansas prairie. He rode the outbound train to small towns to make grocery deliveries, then ran ten or twenty miles home. This was early 1900's, with much land already plowed, but dry upland pastures left to bluestem and cattle. I think of him running, breathing steadily for miles, his breath mixing with quiet heavings of grass.

And in the fall he still ran those miles back to town, a small man among the six-foot stems. Spikes of seeds ripened, and sky filled with flocks. Around him bluestem turned rosy orange, a hue taken from summer sunsets. All winter, long after ornamental maple leaves in town lawns were forgotten, the tallgrass prairie still smoldered with color as he breathed and ran.

Panic Grass, *Dichanthelium acuminatum*

The grasses have their own flowering: spikes of green buds quick to ripen and fill with seeds. Panic grass of the western prairie was a crop, like amaranth.

One small brush of panic grass grows at the corner of my transplanted sod, furred seeds ready to disperse into August drought and long waitfulness, inconspicuous as sparrows.

Sedge Grass

A sedge, triangular stemmed, not yet identified. I wait for the seed plume to emerge from swollen stem to learn its given name.

Star Grass, *Hypoxis hirsuta*

On May Day, hidden within a bluestem clump, the bladed leaves are barely distinguishable from grass—just a bit softer and more deeply hued. The petite blossom of six petals is a miniature daisy beneath a canopy of taller stems. It grows in deep shade, like a woodland flower, but tiny under grass instead of tree trunks.

Like a crocus, it springs whole from the underground. It is invisible from outside the forest of grass, living within a margin of roots and air. It distills a saturated sun yellow, pure passion of yellow.

Hardly anyone knows it is there.

Mushroom, *Basidiomycota*

After days of spring rain, I examine, eye to ground, a clump of chartreuse shoots. I unexpect-edly focus on a miniscule mushroom, smaller than a little fingertip but proportioned exactly as an adult. It has toad skin, bumpy and white as death.

Out of this clump of grasses and flowers comes a cryptic message from below. Perhaps it is edible, perhaps hallucinogenic, perhaps poisonous. It may disappear for years or return quickly this autumn after cold rainstorms.

Red Clover, *Trifolium pratensis*

Red clover, an immigrant, adapted well to a large sky and constant winds. Leaves are split in three parts, or four, to bend easily.

Clusters of three leaves are like three-petalled flowers, green outlined by white chevrons. The actual blossoms are pink confetti. Only bumble bees and a few butterflies have tongues long enough to reach into their depths.

Yellow and black striped bees quiver among blossoms, collecting pollen. Together, bees and red clover create the best honey.

Prairie Phlox, *Phlox pilosa*

A wiry stem holds leaves carefully balanced up the length to clusters of squared-off stars. Each spring the phlox plants take elements out of sediments and turn themselves brilliant magenta.

I remember seeing pink drifts along the banks of the Neosho River, near the Santa Fe Trail crossing. It was late May, and hundred of birds sent songs into the wind during their travel season. The continent's flyway, the Santa Fe Trail, Main Street, and the river all converged there, and also the meandering pathway of pink flowers, electric, like energy running from eyes to the heart.

Groundsel, *Senecio aureus*

Butterweed, cocashweed, coughweed, false valerium, female regulator, golden groundsel, golden ragwort, golden senecio, liferoot, ragwort, wild valerian—this plant takes many names as it grows in damp hollows of grasslands or around ponds and rivers.

With two sets of leaves, groudsel is a shape shifter. One set, oval shaped, grows closest to the rhizomes. They are rounded spoons, smooth, even plain. Stems carry some of these aloft like kites, while the rest cover the ground.

The second set grows topmost like fringed banners, long and deeply notched. The fancywork will frame spring blooms.

Seedlings

The dirt holds in its surface seeds from even more plants, probably sprouting here because of the lack of competition. Near the end of the growing season, I see more possibilities: tiny leaf rosettes; a lambs quarter seedling; an anonymous shoot of cordate leaflets; and a single leaf of vetch. The two-inch start of vetch has paired leaf parts up and down the vein, its delicate shape coming into being while warm air still surrounds it.

The clump of Elkins Prairie, three feet deep, also has within it roots cut off by the plow blade.

Bluestem grasses grow roots ten to twelve feet deep or more, so this season the roots must be groping toward limestone bedrock of our hillside.

II.
ELKINS PRAIRIE: THE SECOND YEAR

The spiky goldenrod came up early within the tangle of yellow stems, in the same spot as last year, but more profusely. The rabbit-eared leaves emerged in thick circles. Other plants were slower to green up, and more sparse. By May, thick stems of goldenrod leaves filled the clump of original prairie; they reached out to open plot of garden space.

The other large plant turned out to be fleabane, not groundsel. The vigorous, branched plant braced itself against the back fence. It grew as big as a small tree and bloomed from June to September—tiny daisies sprinkled over twiggy stems. As some flowerlets wilted and turned into seed fuzz, others on the same stem bloomed.

Grasses never developed full size in the unusually cool weather. Day after day of May and June and even July were cloudy. Rain fell almost every day. Only the little bluestem appeared, not the turkey-foot bluestem that grew to six feet the first season.

I told my neighbors Betsy and Leslie Evans about the aggressive goldenrod and stunted bluestem, and they said wildflowers need the competition of grasses to keep from overgrowth. They had mowed their wildflower patch after a disappointing season, and the next year, within grass, the flowers did better than ever. I pondered whether to take out some of the goldenrod or mow the patch or burn it next year, like ranchers burn the Flint Hills each spring. I decided to let the plants find their own balance in the artificial environment of my garden.

The prairie phlox bloomed brilliant fuchsia in May, but it was hidden by the fence. I wanted to cut the flower stalk for the kitchen table, but also I did not want to alter the plant's cycle. I left it alone and visited it every day, pulling away leaves around it. The foliage increased all summer, and then turned to a lemon yellow at the end of the year.

The mushroom did not reappear.

The surprise was star grass, a petite plant hidden under leaves of other plants. I had never seen it before and searched books for information. Finally, a friend knew of star grass from Japanese gardening, where the five-inch plant is individually potted and admired. One morning, alone, I lifted goldenrod leaves and bluestem grass to observe one bloom. The blossom, similar to a star-of-Bethlehem blossom, was a deep hue of yellow.

All spring I searched for the blue aster, which was still vivid in my mind from the fall before. It had lasted a month, into light frosts, and was a spectacular five-foot plant. This August a small replica appeared, never upright, but sprawled and crippled by goldenrod stalks. But outside the original prairie clump, mixed in with parsley and lettuce, two white asters appeared, also small, probably offspring of the first blue aster.

In September the goldenrod finally bloomed, but stems had uncoiled all over the ground and were hard to see at any distance. Still, the bronze crowns of petals were visible to bees and butterflies. I noticed stands of goldenrod on drives to the country, and

clearly the natural size was much smaller than my garden. They were three feet tall, not six feet, and upright, not sprawling. Although the clump we saved from the original Elkins Prairie preserved many species of plants, still this is not a natural place for them. Next year I could plant lettuce around the clump or native grass to more closely imitate their natural situation, like elephants in a zoo cage with rocky pools and scattered forage. But should I give over more space to the prairie plants or maintain the patch for tomatoes and domesticated basil?

The afternoon before first frost, October 18, red clover bloomed fresh in thin sun. I snapped off dried stems, and I noticed new goldenrod leaves still emerging, tough and bright green.

III.
THE THIRD YEAR: THE INTELLIGENCE OF PLANTS

In June I began to understand intelligence in a new way—not just as calculations in the human brain, but rather as any meaningful expression of patterns.

I realized intelligence could exist in different locations in my body—places I would not normally experience consciousness—and if this were possible, then a kind of intelligence could exist in the body of a plant.

I learned this new attitude after a series of healings with an acupuncturist: these were sessions where energy flowed out of nerve points in my deep muscles and bones. During the same time as these healings, I noticed a new species, a compass plant, growing in the center of the Elkins Prairie tract in my garden. I understood how its leaves embodied a kind of intelligence, which directed its leaves to align north to south. This is not unlike my own cellular-level intelligence, which keeps my complex body systems alive.

Another small miracle was the appearance of this new species after three growing seasons. Perhaps I overlooked the seedling plant the first years, but now it was a tough, spiny adult. Its long leaves, shaped somewhat like oak leaves, endured all summer.

I noticed the compass plant as though it were an individual being. The plant was small, with only three leaves rising out of the ground and unsupported by any stalk. At first the most upright leaf would slant east, but over the weeks it began to grow more northward. I had an unusual sense of personality with the plant, a sense of its individuality as distinct from others of its kind. It seemed assertive. It had the unconscious strength of a teenager during a growth spurt, and this was expressed in its upright bristles, leathery leaves, and in its determined orientation to the magnetic pole. The central vein of each leaf bulged like the vein in the forearm of a strong man.

In the mass of miniature prairie, stiff goldenrod leaves grew in profusion, along with bluestem grasses, but as the season continued, the obtrusive goldenrod leaves splayed out around the compass plant leaves like an enormous, six-foot wreath. The new plant established its place in the foliage, as the centerpiece. There seemed to be an agreement among the species to make room for the newcomer. The strength of its personality was that strong.

The year of 1993 had record rains, including twenty inches in July, due to volcanic eruption in the

Philippines and an active El Niño cycle in the Pacific Ocean. Perhaps this explains the appearance of a new species after three growing seasons. Or maybe it had hidden throughout the previous seasons underneath the more aggressive plants, gathering its strength.

Rain also nourished an aster plant, which grew as big as a shrub against the back of the garden. It rivaled the size of an ashy sunflower next to it, and both collapsed from their own weight before August.

Brilliant pink phlox bloomed inconspicuously, shaded by larger leaves, but I remembered to look for it. Its fuchsia was a discharge of energy as intense as a lost memory.

The young compass plant continued to turn its leaves to point the way to the north star. It knew exactly how to grow, how to express its knowledge in every gesture of its life.

Making Garden

My mother told me women who garden know how to accept their aging. They know the life cycles, birth to death. I remember she told me this in Mrs. Soden's walled garden, in May, as lilies of the valley scented the air. I was in junior high, not aware of the trajectory of time I would travel, nor the gardens I would plant when I was grown. I accepted her words as truth. I was on the verge of womanhood myself, but with no real understanding of what that meant. Many springtimes later I came to understand the blessing of a childhood spent among gardens.

The tradition of prairie gardens was an uncelebrated blessing. My love of plants comes from two accidents of birth. I was born in a small town surrounded by tallgrass prairie, and I was born to a mother who kept a garden.

Hundreds of plant species grow in Lyon County, at the edge of the Flint Hills. The Hills are one of the last remaining stands of unplowed prairie in the country, and grasses are only the most visible flora. Along gullies, woody sumac turns scarlet in October, and wild indigo blues the hillsides in spring. Each season brings new waves of color. In early spring, the green growth begins as a lime shading and progresses to full-blown emerald green in May. Even winter has its colors—maroons mixed with yellows. One color scheme seems to predominate for awhile, and then another takes its place, and another.

Tuberous plants, grasses, shrubby plants, shallow-rooted and deep-rooted plants, mushrooms, and bulbs all grow in balance with each other. They space themselves across the ground to use sun and water as well as possible. These plants embody their own forms of intelligence: compass plant leaves always align with North; sunflowers follow the daily route of the sun. Some plants give off chemical herbicides to repel competitors from their territory.

As a child, I did not notice as remarkable this expanse of virgin prairie. When we drove in the country, or when I looked out west of town, the land was just there. Brilliant and subtle colors soaked into my imagination not as acquired knowledge, but as the framework for thought itself. As people in northern countries have many words for snow, I had a large palette of colors I never thought about twice. In a box of sixty-four crayons, I looked for missing hues because I needed more to color the world as I knew it.

Countryside was distinct from the town since there were no houses and yards, but it was not completely separate. Every vacant lot on my block reverted back to wilderness if left unmowed. The pattern of streets was interrupted by resurgences of prairie in unweeded yards, drainage ditches, and even cracks in the red brick streets. Especially in August drought, the edges of gardens filled with tough native plants while tender flowers dried out.

In the summers I spent hours, even days, in a vacant lot nearby. Stiff grass reached all around and over my head, and I felt as though I were walking through a huge bird's nest. Within the grass I could see nothing but stems and sky, and all I could hear was the rustling of thin leaves. A wild plum tree grew at the back of the lot, as well as a small forest of pokeberry and sumac. There, within city limits, I experienced the strength of all those plants adapted to high winds and all extremes of temperatures. I became acquainted with the substance of the prairies.

Garden plants were another experience. They were consciously planted, fertilized, watered, weeded, and cut for flower arrangements. As a youngster, I knew I was expected to learn these skills.

Most garden flowers came to the prairies with European immigrants—my assorted great-great-grandparents. From the old country they brought notions of English and continental gardening. The climate allowed certain adaptations of roses, daisies, daffodils, lilies, and tulips. Land was plentiful, so townspeople cultivated spacious yards according to heritage and whim. I remember a side yard of bachelor buttons, all shades of lavender and pink; a collection of hybridized iris; hedges of voluptuous peonies; and ferns along a house foundation. I loved the exotic sense created by each garden. And these gardens were to be shared. During iris season, neighbors came by our house to observe particular blossoms as they would visit a family with a new baby: Gingerbread Boy was beige with teal stripes; Dundee was powder white with blue-stippled plicata. My mother also hybridized some seedlings, so she would wait each April for the unfolding of new combinations of hues.

Yard ornaments added personal touches, like knick knacks in living rooms. There were stone Japanese lanterns and shiny globes that reflected the sun. Ceramic toads and turtles were commonplace, and as they weathered, they gained an organic authenticity. Low picket fences marked boundaries from one section of a garden to another.

On one walk to a distant neighborhood, I once found a back yard with a red and blue totem pole that stood ten feet high. Six sets of eyes stared at me. I was so used to surreal sights in people's yards that I did not think it unusual. The grotesque faces blended naturally into a stand of hollyhocks and red petunias.

My mother gardened with single-minded fervor. She planted a willow and a maple and floribunda rosebushes named, by coincidence, with her maiden named Cecil Bruner; by coincidence, her maiden name was also Bruner. The name of the rose sounded naturally in my ear like names of uncles or cousins. She planted hens-and-chickens outside my window, and grape hyacinths and iris.

Feathery asparagus grew in the back garden, behind the grapevines and strawberries, and this was a special place of seclusion where my mother would disappear indefinitely. It was like an extra room in the house, just shut off in winter months. I liked the sense of enclosure behind the curtain of grape vines, like in the grassy vacant lot.

Through the years my mother worked the yard over from one end to the other as purposefully as she rearranged furniture. She dug out a level surface and laid shale flagstones for a patio. She raised beds and dug out drainage ditches. In springtime she sheared overgrown clumps of violets or daisies and gave them to the neighbors. She inventoried the yard to see which plants had died in the spells of zero weather. In the summer she checked to make sure flowers had metal tags with names printed in black grease. In the fall she brought out bushel baskets to fill with leaves for the compost pile.

Every morning she walked through the yard to see which flowers would bloom that day, from snow-drops in March to chrysanthemums in October.

She taught me unusual names for plants: coreop-sis, hyacinth, ajuga, coleus, phlox, flax, vinca, narcis-sus, caladium, trillium. I also learned ordinary names: honeysuckle, spearmint, lemon balm, jack-in-the-pulpit, forget-me-not.

In her seventies she still has a collection of a hun-dred some iris and over two hundred day lilies, each with a name, "Towhead" and "Hearts of Fire" and "Cream Delight" and "Day Queen."

*

When I set up housekeeping in my first home, a small house in Lawrence, I chopped my first garden out of the grass sod. In those politically conscious times, the early 1970's, I decided to grow only what we could eat. I prepared a small plot for corn, onions, potatoes, and soybeans. But I did not realize that legacies of two garden traditions came with the house. Like it or not, there were extensive flower gardens packed into the lot, all around the house. And across the alley lived an elderly woman who would oversee the vegetable patch before the first radish ripened.

The woman who owned the house before us was a retired school teacher, one of those orderly types. She must have arranged plants like rows of chairs in a classroom. Though I never met her, she left a chart of each flowerbed for me, drawn to scale and with instructions for care. The real estate agent must have told her I was young, because she wrote out details of everything, from pruning back roses to separating clumps of chrysanthemums and iris. She had prim-roses—temperamental exotica in the drought-prone Midwest—and a fencing of large tiger lilies across the side yard. At an age when I wanted to establish my own identity, I found myself in another woman's garden, complete with primroses.

All of this would have been wonderful if my life were to follow the slower speed of the previous owner's life. But I was in another generation, and I had stubborn ideas about organic food as a value over ornamental flowers. And I was finishing a masters degree in American literature. At the same time my husband was working on a law degree, we were both working part time, and we had two children in eighteen months. Especially after the second baby, I entered into a state of permanent exhaustion. I was not to have a night's sleep for three or four years. Nonetheless, I expected myself to be a good-natured mother, wife, daughter, in-law, sister, neighbor, shopper, house cleaner, graduate student, teacher—and gardener. Fortunately, I was young.

I knew that if I did not water and weed and prune and divide clumps of roots, that the plants would die. The beautiful flowers were a burden as well as a legacy from that woman I never met. Those years were a blur, and now, looking back, I can appreciate

that her invisible presence was part of my instruction about gardening. I saw how she selected flowers for different parts of the yard, depending on the sun. Not only were there obvious considerations of shade or full sun, but certain plants do better in morning sun, and others, like succulent moss roses, can tolerate the full blast of the afternoon sun in July and August. I saw how she massed many plants of the same color together—an island of blood-red mums or a stretch of shasta daisies along the property line. She knew how to show off delicate fronds of coral bells, next to the back door, or single specimens like one magnificent yellow-rose-of-Texas bush that punctuated the corner of the house. She had planted a showy ginkgo tree along the front walk, with fan-shaped green leaves that all fell at once, overnight, in the fall. She must have had the leisure to savor all this in the years before me.

I wish I had had time to appreciate it all—to tend it carefully. Instead, we put up an inexpensive wire fence for the children. We found an old tire and filled it with sand from the riverbanks for a sandpile. I watered when I could. This was a prophetic pattern: I have never had time to tend a garden as I wish.

*

The other woman who entered my life with that house was Naomi Hardesty, a woman in her seventies who had farmed in northern Kansas. She had retired from her wheatfields to a frame house directly in back of the garden spot of my new yard. Naomi was my link to the traditions of country people, the pioneers who came west in covered wagons. I had not known anyone like her.

In small towns when I was growing up, there was a separation between townspeople and farmer people. Each group held the other in polite disdain. I did not understand these undercurrents as a child; I just knew that country western music was unacceptable, and education was the highest good. We grew up with the Sunday *New York Times, Readers Digest* condensed novels, dozens of paperbacks, and the *New Yorker.* These, and regular music lessons, were cul-

ture. People on farms, or country people, did not have these advantages. Willa Cather delineates this division between immigrant farmers and more settled townspeople in *My Antonia,* and there the country people are much more attractive, embodied in Antonia's glistening brown eyes and rich family life. But at the age of twenty-three, I had not read *My Antonia,* and I had not been afforded the chance to meet anyone like Mrs. Hardesty.

She was born on a farm around the turn of the century, when over ninety percent of the United States population lived in rural areas. She was a living fossil of the displacements of that time. She lived in a different world from what she learned as a child, especially in a college town, and she was glad to see, finally, some sensible neighbors turn over a garden.

Over the next three years I learned about her life. She had married a kind man, and they farmed and raised cattle together. He became ill and was bedridden for years, so she had the responsibilities of both the cattle and the household. They rented out the wheatfields to tenants. She told me she used to knit and stitch embroidery on horseback while she tended the cattle. She must have worked very hard, especially with a dying man to nurse. After her husband died, and after she became too old to live alone in the country, she moved to Lawrence to be near her sister and her brother-in-law, whom she loved. Tenants still worked her lands a hundred miles west, and they sent crop money after the wheat harvests. She lived on that stipend plus a job as a companion for an elderly woman. One July she gave all of her wheat profits to her church for a stained glass window, and to set an example for the congregation to be generous.

Because of her husband's illness, Mrs. Hardesty never had children, and she was very fond of her nieces and nephews. She became very attached to my two sons as they arrived in the world. She babysat for me, and I was too young and desperate to question whether she should be doing such difficult work at her age. I gladly accepted the help.

She never talked specifically about gardening on her farm. That was taken for granted.

That first spring she watched us, her new neighbors, dig up our lawn for our first garden, and therefore she approved of us. We were behaving in the proper manner. On fragile legs, she made her way across the alley to make our acquaintance. Thereafter, whenever she saw us outdoors, she felt welcome to come visit. I have to admit that sometimes I was outdoors for a moment of solitude during the babies' afternoon naptime, and I was not always happy to see her. I just wanted to doze in the lawn chair. But I also knew that when the clouds threatened a tornado, I was welcome in her basement.

One time she brought me several dozen starts of houseplants. She had observed I had none, and did what she thought was the right thing to help out a newlywed. I did my best to act grateful, though all I could see was more work and more messes for my sons and the cats. Those were the days we had to clean off the kitchen table completely even before dinner was over, so human and feline climbers would not stick knees in the butter or fists in the jam. Of course, Mrs. Hardesty had no idea. And I learned to love the mother-in-law tongues, philodendrums and violets—and her lesson of generosity.

The most wonderful thing about her gardening vocabulary was the way she expressed the words "to make garden." To me this sounded like love, an ongoing process. With two babies at my side as I made garden, and sometimes Mrs. Hardesty too, this was appropriate for the process of generations. To plant seeds and after a time reap vegetables is a mystery—as much as birth and time.

We grew sweet corn, green beans, lettuce, peas and potatoes. I did not know that corn left on the stalks becomes starchy and dried out, until Mrs. Hardesty mentioned she had trouble getting her false teeth through the gift corn. We learned the unexpected pleasure of digging potatoes. The vining foliage and small white flowers do not suggest tubers will form below ground. In early summer we dug gingerly around the plants and found dirt-covered lumps. Cleaned and boiled, they indeed tasted like *pommes des terres*, apples of the earth. Peas, too,

were now a much different experience from produce in a grocery store, as we spent hours by the television shelling succulent peas out of the pods. My mother-in-law gave me seeds for Chinese green beans a yard long, bitter melons, winter melons, and musty smelling Chinese parsley. These were curiosities to our neighbor, and she graciously tested each one.

Mrs. Hardesty kept a close eye on how all our crops were coming, and compared them to her pole-beans-and-lettuce kitchen garden by her back door. She showed me how to sow seeds broadcast style to leave no room for weeds. She must have had a huge garden on the farm, as she knew about every plant. And when I decided to learn how to pickle and can the vegetables, she gave me jars and free advice. She told me about a young child who had been killed when a pressure cooker exploded, so I was terrified every time I operated the contraption, and kept the boys far away. She repeated the story every time she saw the pressure cooker out, so I would not forget to be careful.

Even then I wished I had more time to listen to her stories. I had a sense of what I was missing, by living in my generation of women who expected to be mothers and professionals and everything else. I wish I could say I stayed in touch with her after we moved to another town and when she became infirm in her eighties. I sent Christmas cards several years, took the boys to see her one Halloween, and stayed too busy. I last heard of her when I saw the obituary in the newspaper. She had returned to her farm community at the end, and I imagine she is buried near the pastures she once tended on a horse.

Every spring when I turn the garden into rows of lettuce and tomato plants, I know Naomi Hardesty is with me, making garden. I know her hands moved in the same motions as she sowed green beans and lettuce and corn. I am left with her story. I am left with the half-told story of a retired teacher who loved primroses, and who left me her house. Most of all, I am left with memories of my mother's garden, the backdrop for the story of my entire life.

Sherwood Way

Though surrounded by expanses of undisturbed prairie, the town I grew up in had an atmosphere of human habitation. Houses made up the natural world as far as I, a town kid, could see. A family activity was driving around town and looking at other people's homes. My grandfather loved to do this, and later my mother would take me on drives to see the blooming seasons of daffodils or iris. Details of the neighbors' houses were carefully noted—the porch swings or fencing or yard ornaments. I remember houses from my childhood as vividly as I remember the people.

I live close enough to my hometown to return every month to visit. Even now, houses on Sherwood Street, near my neighborhood, sit like rows of people on a town bus. Though lined up in uniform order, each is a different size or color—with coats of olive or yellow slickers. These cottages and ranch houses and bungalows blend together, none-theless, under the tree canopy, a ceiling of fifty-year-old maples. This is the last variegated neighborhood in town, the last one built before tract housing.

Some houses of whitewashed wood and plaster follow the outlines of Victorian architecture, or Dutch colonial. A few replicate southern plantations in miniature, with Doric columns, and a few are Californian ranchers. At the end of the block is a pure white Southwestern-style house, a stucco box with recessed windows. Porches vary—some are simple patio extensions or triangular stoops—but all are open living rooms with porch swings where a sofa would sit. Each dwelling is an individual, yet somehow the overall look of the neighborhood is harmonious. The sloping streets hold each house in place, and the treeline and yards flow together.

In an odd way I long for certain of these houses, and sometimes rooms within them. One of my mother's friends lives in a house covered with pink pebbles, like jelly beans pressed into a gingerbread house. I drive by to see the house as much as to see the woman. I associate the house so closely with her, along with her dark hair and voice, that the stone pattern is like another embodiment of her personality. I also feel almost affectionate toward another friend's living room with a painting of a jazz bassist, or my piano teacher's parlor with Windsor chairs. I do not covet ownership exactly, but somehow I want to blend into each house, or its essence. These dwellings must represent safe wombs, or safe Edens of order.

Sometimes in dreams these houses drift to other towns where I have lived. Or my age shifts to anywhere from infancy to adulthood, and I still move through the same neighborhood. The houses and brick streets take on mythic meanings in the dream world of nightmares and auguries. Though I do not understand the reason why I select these houses, they are backdrops to important dramas.

One recent Sunday I took my mother out for a drive, and I meandered around the old neighborhood until I found familiar houses, set along slopes and ravines of the subdivision called Sherwood. They were much larger than I remembered, with more sky and sun around them. Streets were wider, with oaks and shrubs and sugar maples along the curbing. I realized I must have telescoped these streets to fit into tiny tableaux of memory. The physical reality was too much to contain. Perhaps I contrasted city scenes to surrounding infinity of prairie lands and wheat fields. Perhaps I needed to reduce vast yards and houses into manageable snapshots for my memory.

I found a favorite house, that of my old piano teacher, and it was chocolate brown, not gray like the picture in my mind. In dreams I always looked out from the porch steps, at a twilight scene fringed by pines. But from the street, the real house seemed a looming part of the ridge it sat on, a set of planes and angles instead of what I remembered as porch and slate roof and bay window. It was flat and lifeless, like a face without expression, like the "brown imperturbable faces" of houses in James Joyce's Dublin. The time I spent on that porch has passed, and the house could just as well be a façade, with empty space behind it. I had no sense of its other dimensions.

That Sunday my mother and I also drove by our old house on Washington Street, where I lived from the ages of five to eighteen. But it had become plain. New owners had removed the spreading cedars that formed walls around the porch. I spent many days in that outdoor playroom with the pungent cedar smell around me, but now the porch was a bare slab with a wrought iron love seat. It looked uncomfortable for lovers or anyone else. And the seedling maple my mother planted years ago towered over the street. Even now, as I write this, I scale down its size, but from the car that day it rose forty feet. The double driveway that had been a basketball court was empty and the hoop shorn from the roof. I looked for the floribunda rose bushes by the side door, to see if these garden landmarks would make the visitation meaningful, but branches blocked the sight. Only my memories can make the house live again. In the car, in the gray autumn light, I could

not evoke any feelings. The house was but a husk of its past. We drove on by.

Yet I know my underlying ideas about the shape of the world come from the time I spent in that house. As a child I loved the sense of height from the second story rooms. I could see a long ways into the horizon from that modest elevation. In the far distance trees made a brushy line against sky. And I still feel comfortable in small, closely connected rooms like those on the ground floor. The layout of the Washington Street house still dictates my own sense of domestic geometry, like a genetic blueprint. I now live in a similar house, where living room, kitchen, and bedrooms are within reach of each other. By instinct, I know my meals will be in a small room with a window and a table. My house will be small enough that I can hear everyone in adjacent rooms and know we are all safe.

I remember winter afternoons when the sun slanted through a small window in the front door. Lemon-colored light reflected on dust specks in the air. The living room vibrated with these tiny prisms, only visible at this hour. The fact of the house's western exposure caused me to have a love of afternoon-lighted rooms, and sunsets and their brilliant colors. It caused me to look to the west for storm clouds or wispy cirrus clouds of cold weather. I feel reflective at that hour, perhaps because I remember my grandfather at prayer against the setting sun, framed by that window.

When I saw the house again, I understood that someone else looked out the west window, and the mute glass refracts light as indifferently for them as it once did for me. In the poem "The West Window," W. S. Merwin describes an old house, "the windows went on with their lives as though they were/separate and outside where each had a sky of its own." Those windows are no longer my eyes on the world—though I still live with the way they shape my expectations of the outdoors for me. They come to life again whenever I see sunset prisms through glass. I have become one of those westerly oriented panes, holding patches of light and shadow.

In my dreams I still merge with walls and ceilings of the breakfast nook, and I become, as well, the ac-tor within. Indeed, the houses and neighborhoods, with their distinct ambiances, are like characters themselves, with different visages than humans, but just as real. My old bedroom, a room I slept in for fifteen years, is mixed into my unconscious. There were pink ballerinas in the wallpaper, and I continue to have good feelings about ballet, even though I have seen fewer than a half dozen performances. Every dancer I see is an archetypal figure from my bedroom walls, come to life. And after waking to the sound of birdcalls all those years, I keep up informal birdwatching wherever I live. When I lived in Chicago briefly I was uncomfortable because we never heard birds at the highrise windows.

Through the years I have lived in a dozen houses, and each is a part of me. Gaston Bachelard explains in *The Poetics of Space* that houses overlap in our minds:

> Through dreams, the various dwelling-places in our lives co-penetrate and retain the treasures of former days. And after we are in the new house, when memories of other places we have lived in

come back to us, we travel to the land of Motionless Childhood, motionless the way all Immemorial Things are.

I have not left the shells of old houses behind, but rather internalize them, layer them one over the other. I have taken remembered images, reduced them, and turned them into shrines of my past. They have become standards of how I expect space to be divided.

On the visit to the old neighborhood, we passed the Washington Street house in just a few moments, and my experience of the house changed. I realized my body no longer has a direct relationship to this neighborhood—but I carry within me the imprint of that house—and of the entire neighborhood of shrubs and brick streets—in the way I perceive spaces and enclosures. A further part of the contract between humans and their houses is a clause of mutual influence. Lance Henson, a poet of Cheyenne heritage, writes of the home where he grew up, "the walls and the floors and the door have a life invested in them which is invested in you . . . there's a certain attach-ment which goes beyond a house and a person living in a house. It really becomes a part of your life force." Whether haphazard or arranged as purposefully as a painting, homes mirror back the energy within. They intertwine with the organisms they house.

My memories are more vivid than houses left in the neighborhood I once called home. These memories began with real objects, but then were abbreviated, with different emphasis of color and size, in ways to fit into my mental drawers. My imagination took these fragments, then, and created new beings. As my mother and I continued our drive that Sunday afternoon, I noticed a few houses were gone, replaced by ranch houses. But the old houses with screened-in porches remain, and the same corner mansions with carriage houses, unaltered from thirty years ago.

I live in another house now, and I know my way around its rooms even in the dark. The walls are as familiar as my own skin. When I dream, its walls are always there, just beyond sight. They merge with the walls of all the places I have ever lived.

At Home on The Range: The Kansas Vernacular in Literature

Recently I heard a Southern writer, Henry Taylor, read poetry at a Midwest writers conference. He is a well-spoken Virginian who won the Pulitzer several years back. I remembered meeting him at a national conference—and chitchatting about American University where he teaches and about the writers on the dance floor. This year, as I listened to him read, I noticed rural topics similar to those in my own poetry, but articulated in a totally different *voice*. He has that soft Atlantic Coast-Southern accent, and I speak with hard rrr's and some nasal twang. He layers stories and descriptions and histories; I strive for vivid images that resonate within the reader, with the apparatus of my artifice submerged. Still, we share a similar background: he grew up on a farm, and I grew up near farms and ranches, in Emporia, Kansas. Emporia is semi-rural, so the cycles of plants, animals and weather are still a daily rhythm.

Taylor read poems about subjects familiar to me—blackberry picking, tractors, and horses. He read the poem "Breakings," from *An Afternoon of Pocket Billiards*:

Long before I first left home, my father
tried to teach me horses, land, and sky,
to show me how his kind of work was done.
I studied how to be my father's son,
but all I learned was, when the wicked die,
they ride combines through barley forever.

Every summer I hated my father
as I drove hot horses through dusty grass;
and so I broke with him, and left the farm
for other work, where unfamiliar weather
broke on my head an unexpected storm
and things I had not studied came to pass.

So nothing changes, nothing stays the same,
and I have returned from a broken home
alone, to ask for a job breaking horses.
I watch a colt on a long line making
tracks in dust, and think of the kinds of breakings
there are, and the kinds of restraining forces.

Though rural, this is not poetry written in my native tongue. Taylor writes in the Southern style—based on storytelling, with timing and an underlying sense of narrative—and that ability to turn a phrase. This poem is a story of divorce and failed families. In addition, there is that repertoire of aphorisms in the dialect, like "when the wicked die" and "nothing changes, nothing stays the same." My father's mother was from Texas, and I remember colorful expressions that occasionally punctuated his usual Kansas dialect—sayings like "He was as busy as a one-armed paper hanger." (I never heard my completely Kansan mother use phrases like this.) In Taylor's public reading of "Riding a One-Eyed Horse" and "Landscape with Tractor," he intermingled droll wit and an ornate descriptive ability. It was a practiced reading of fine work that I admire like I admire many Irish and many French writers—and like them, Taylor also writes in a language foreign to me.

Listening to Taylor gave me the idea to try a definition of something to me that is as unremarkable as the taste of water or the smell of air—a description of Kansas vernacular language. This is not an easily measured quality, but still as distinct as Taylor's accent from mine. Despite our shared academic training in British and American poetics, and despite a shared experience of country life, our voices are different. The authenticity of our work comes not from what we learned in school, but from what we learned at our mothers' knees. There is a distinctive local speech pattern, and I recognize it most when I contrast it to the speech of out-of-staters. I recognize the "other-ness" of various American English dialects. Then I turn to Kansas-bred writers like Robert Day, Harley Elliott, Steven Hind, and William Stafford—and Stephen Meats, Tom Averill, and Fred Whitehead—to hear echoes of my mother tongue.

I am aware of how imprecise is an attempt to delineate a Midwestern voice. Do I start with linguistic tables and then match them up with writers who fit? What about Kansas writers who have grown up elsewhere? What are the linguistic variations within Kansas? Linguists note a line that runs across the middle of the state. Dozens of problems arise. Still, I will suggest some ideas based on personal experience, just as writers like Pat C. Hoy generalize about the southern voice, and Gerald Vizenor, Kim Blaeser, Kathryn Shanley write about a Native American aesthetic. I will toss out some ideas based on publications by several Kansas-bred writers, just to open the discussion.

*

My favorite example of a few, well-chosen words is from the artist Stan Herd, who grew up in Protection, Kansas. His father farmed many years next to a widow woman, and they exchanged occasional neighborly gestures, like returning runaway cattle.

But they hardly saw each other for months at a time. When the woman was preparing to retire to town, she stopped Stan's father in the road one day, as their cars passed each other, and she informed him she intended to leave her farm to him. That brief conversation was the only discussion of the issue, and when she died, indeed her farm was left to the Herd family.

Kansans are masters of understatement. Robert Day, from Merriam, Kansas, has made an icon of the terse rancher he worked for in Hays, Kansas. He immortalized Ward Sullivan as the character Spangler in *The Last Cattle Drive*. The facts of Ward's life make it clear that the character is not exaggerated, but if anything toned down. In the book, Spangler has brief dialogues with the narrator, who is a lot like the young Robert Day:

"What are all those lumps up and down the lane there?"

"Cow shit."

"I see."

and further, the rancher educates the young University of Kansas graduate:

"How come Jed doesn't talk to me?"
"He doesn't like you."
"I see."

"Am I going to need a horse?"
"Can you ride?"
"No."
"I don't think you'll need a horse."

The language is not in itself entertaining, like a Southerner's use of figures of speech, but rather the situation is made funny by the understated emphasis of the obvious: humans live in a state of ignorance. I have heard Day tell stories about the real man Sullivan shooting out his television and allegedly growing millions of dollars of marijuana on his ranch, and further stories about legendary fights with his wife, who once drove Sullivan's truck through a downtown storefront as a retaliatory gesture. Sullivan/Spangler, like his wife, was a person of action, and whatever he said he would do, he did. In the book, Spangler says he will drive his cattle to Kansas City himself rather than pay exorbitant trucking fees, and he does. In real life Ward Sullivan never replaced his television. It was dead for good. The action spoke for itself, and there was no florid eulogy.

Day's short stories, like "Speaking French in Kansas" and "Edith of the Eighth Street Tavern," celebrate the atmosphere of small town communities in the vernacular of the inhabitants. He is a smart writer, with postmodernist techniques when appropriate, but all his fiction centers on characters like Huck Finn—rebels with good hearts. They represent the great tradition of the Kansas individualist. Unlike Huck, their speech is distilled to the fewest possible words.

Another master of the Kansas vernacular is poet Harley Elliott of Salina. Elliott has published over eleven books of poetry. His most recent writing project is a narrative about flint, especially the kinds used by Native Americans for projectile points. He can identify where each kind of flint comes from, as well as the mode of manufacture. This is not a commercial project, but a continuation of his years spent walking the banks of prairie creeks as he looks for arrow heads. His writing grows from his life.

This Kansas poet's lines read as smoothly as talk at the local coffee shop—where he does spend time. He writes unpretentiously in "Stopping to Piss at Night":

The great fish pause in
southern river water

for the man who stops in the night
with darkness at each elbow.

It's then the stars breathe
down our necks the most.
Cars idle on while

staring at our sleepy boots
we leak into the earth and

stop alert as catfish:
dark air for a moment
flew over our bones. (Darkness at Each Elbow)

Again, the vocabulary—aside from "piss" in the title—is ordinary, and maybe even "piss" is ordinary outside the pages of poetry books. Catfish are unremarkable, unheroic fish, aside from their whiskers. The car doesn't roar or whine or say anything dramatic; it just "idles." Yet in the most humble of human gestures, pissing at roadside, the totality of the cosmos comes together, from stars to earth The man has a satori-like moment of recognition here. There is a similar self-deprecatory humor—as with Day and William Stafford—based on the perspective of the small role of humans within the immensity of the universe.

Denise Low

Here's another one of my favorite Elliott poems, "Secret Lover in the Laundromat":

Somewhere during
the whirlpool cycle
I feel my heart
nearing your lap

you are reading an article
on supersonic flight:
I am staring
at an ad for margarine

and George Washingtons bright
blue eyes
stand up on a million quarters
when your whispering nylons cross.

Why not love
in the laundromat after all?
Shall I offer to unload
your dryer plunging fingers
in to warm clothes

like a butcher
before a great carcass?

Will the problems of margarine
and speed of light
find resolution in our time?

A solitary crow crosses
the falling snow outside
and you look into my eyes:
a blue-eyed scream of plastic butter
crossing a brown-eyed
scream of falling planes.

You sigh.
I blow my nose.
Our love is doomed.   (The Secret Lover Poems)

Elliott makes fun of himself as he flounders in the throes of the most ridiculous aspect of the human condition—mating. Tricks of the various tropes are stripped away, so that the rhetorical attention focuses upon the immediate situation like a spotlight. The topic is paramount, not the sensibility of the writer. Elliott is not an obvious juggler of words, like Henry Taylor, but an observer who keeps his own voice hidden within the immediacy of experience.

*

Steven Hind, a poet who grew up in the Flint Hills, calls his style of indirect writing "that trick of silence." The phrase illustrates the quiet voice of the plainsman, as well as a surrender to the mystery of the world he lives in:

That Trick of Silence

This slab of land, never
So much anything in the public
Mind as a place to get behind you
From Kansas City to Denver,
Was just out there, out where
So little stood upright past
The hundredth meridian
That every tree was remarkable,
Every stream a new chance
You could not have predicted.
You could drink and wash
Your face and look around
Where the vast nothing held open
Its face to teach you that
Trick of silence.

There is an acknowledgment of the low opinion most people have of the western plains; no longer called the Great American Desert, this is now flyover country, or a "slab of land." The poem recapitulates the European-American experience of the plains, with the demarcation of the one-hundredth meridian and the longing for trees. A water source—the "new chance" of "every stream"—was critical to the settlers, as well as the Native peoples before. And Hind makes clear the reason for the self-deprecatory attitude of the Midwesterner, yet the narrator turns to the emptiness that is his home and finds a spiritual dimension. It is not an orthodox Christianity of his heritage, but more akin to the idea of *wakan*, from the Lakota, the idea of mystery. Like many desert-like landscapes, this place too, this "vast nothing," teaches its own religion.

Hind has less of the humor of Day or Elliott, but his language shares with Elliott the same relationship to direct speech. He does not use music in his writing like a Southerner, and the rhythms and vocabulary are simple. A few of the words have a Latin etymology, like "meridian," but rather the one-syllable Anglo-Saxon words like "stream" and "tree" and "land" and "wash" and "vast" are the important ones. The limestone stratum that underlies the state is like a "slab." Infinity is the ultimate point of the poem, and this is an abstraction that parallels the landscape. The form fits the content, and the narrator again does not entertain us with complexities of verse—the human invention—but rather covers his traces, so the Germanic tribal origins of language convey action directly—not in latinate borrowings into the mother lode of the English language.

*

Poet William Stafford embodies the archetype of the Kansas writer. This nationally known writer, who won the National Book Award and many other honors, grew up in Kansas during the Depression. He represents not just the typical, but the ideal of the Midwestern character. In a humble fashion, he worked hard and achieved outward success. He hid a shrewd academic intelligence, creating his own philosophy of words.

Kansas was never far removed from Stafford's writing. His son, Kim Stafford, also a writer, recently spoke in Kansas City (Edgar Wolfe Award ceremony, April 9, 1994) about his father, and affirmed that the poet had never left Kansas—meaning in his attitudes and language—though he wrote on many subjects. Stafford often harkens back to the Kansas towns he lived in—Hutchinson, Pratt, Wichita—and the landscape he learned throughout his childhood and young adulthood. In fact, he never moved away from Kansas until he was about thirty, when he was driven out by his political stand against war. He was a conscientious objector during World War II, and his son said he left Kansas mostly because there were hard feelings against his politics. This is the down side to people who have firm convictions.

Stafford remained true to his type, and perhaps homely Midwesterners like him represent all rural Americans. They are remnants of the majority of Americans who used to live in rural areas during the early twentieth century and before. Wes Jackson, of the Land Institute in Salina, speculates that this is why many people denigrate country people and Midwesterners in general. Try going to New York or California and telling people you are from Kansas. Woody on *Cheers* is your stereotype. Most families left rural life behind in the last few generations, and in the paradigm of progress—the Turner hypothesis—the past is to be improved on, like each new model of car.

Stafford was as hard working as a farmer. Every morning he awoke at four and wrote. Writer and editor Stephen Meats, from Concordia, says that Stafford was in many ways an ordinary man. He was indeed intelligent and talented, according to Meats, but most of all he did not promote himself as a romantic genius, but rather set about his writing as his vocation in life, no better or worse than any other. In an interview Stafford said, "Everybody has the potential to be a poet," and "It seems I've been writing poetry all my life, since I was a kid. Most people quit. I never did" (*The Oregonian*). He

wanted to build the best possible poems; and if he had been a carpenter, he would have built sturdy houses.

My first personal encounter with Stafford was in 1977, when Mike Smetzer solicited poems for the *Cottonwood Review*. As a new associate editor, I was amazed to see a poet of his stature send a group of poems that was uneven, and Smetzer, the editor, rejected some of them. All the correspondence from the poet was courteous, despite rejection. Some years later I would hear Stafford say in a reading, "Editors are our friends. They save us from publishing bad poems." He always understood his possible fallibility as a writer, and this attitude was apparent when I corresponded with him about the collection I edited, *Kansas Poems of William Stafford*. In 1989 he wrote me, "I'm glad the Kansas poems project is rolling—how I hope my poems will provide you with a worthy text." This is from a man who had won national awards and published with Harper and Row for decades. When our project was nearly completed, he wrote, "Your packet of material makes me feel great. I'd like to deserve such care and insight as you offer." Note the humble "like to deserve" here, the suggestion that he did not deserve any remarkable attention. He was just another worker in the fields of the Lord. As a child I remember my father worrying that I might grow up to be "swell-headed," apparently one of the worst fates for a Kansan, and here I saw Stafford keeping a proper attitude throughout his life, despite a national reputation.

Most of all, Stafford was a deeply spiritual man—but not in an orthodox sense. He transcended the religion of "One Home," which he describes, "Plain black hats rode the thoughts that made our code./ We sang hymns in the house; the roof was near God." His involvement with the simple faith of the Friends, or Quakers, was an essential part of his life. Judith Kitchen writes about this aspect of Stafford's work:

> Imagination is so essential that it leads to a nearly religious experience. Something exists beyond human comprehension; imagination puts man in touch with that larger possibility. Perhaps

the most difficult concept to understand in the work of William Stafford is this religious moment. Although Stafford has no formal religion, the poems contain many words associated with the Quaker faith.

This spiritual life is apparent not only in the language, but also in the confidence of his poetic voice. With ease, he aims for universal truths in his poems. With the simplest words—like "forever," "still," and "sky"—he evokes the largest ideas. "The Little Girl by the Fence at School" ends with

> *And that was the morning someone's heart stopped*
> *and all became still. A girl said, 'Forever?'*
> *And the grass: 'Yes. Forever.' While the sky—*
> *The sky—the sky—the sky.*

*

Sometimes the language of a Kansas writer is highly compressed, like in traditional Native American song lyrics. Lance Henson, a poet of Cheyenne heritage from Calumet, Oklahoma, writes bilingual texts of pithy, highly evocative lines. Sometimes only six short lines long, the poems/songs come from the peyote tradition, he says, where each word is charged with ritual significance. An example is "vision song":

> *the scent of sage and sweetgrass*
> *braids*
> *a man saying goodbye*
> *to himself*

Sage, sweetgrass, and braids have many levels of meaning to an audience familiar with the Cheyenne ways. Braiding of hair, for example, is a daily gesture that recapitulates religious beliefs. To a readership used to the "what you see is what you get" mentality of computers, there is little beyond the literal meaning. Indeed, cultural connotations are lost to most people. Some of Hind's and Stafford's poems share the use of highly connotative vocabulary, which requires a readership willing to travel the territory.

A provocative idea is the extent of the impact of Native Americans on European settlers of the prairies. Was there a blending of the various traditions? Certainly intermarriage occurred often, and in southern Kansas I grew up with many people of mixed heritage. Stafford had some Native American background, as he once told me in a letter: "About our Indianness, yes, my father used to remind me that we had some Indian background, and he always made me feel near to it. Together we read, camped, and Indianed around. . . ." In Kansas a cultural practice transmitted from Native Americans to European-Americans is the spring burning of prairie grasses. This borrowing is documented in a settler's diary from the 1860's, and the practice continues to this day, unbroken for thousands of years.

Solid proof of plains Indians influencing Kansas cultures—and writers—would be difficult to find, but it is possible to speculate. Some experiences of Kansas rural life, like Native American cultures, are obscure outside of the region. I did not fully understand one of Steven Hind's poems about pasture burning, "Fireline," until I experienced the sight of an entire skyline on fire. Like Native American cultures, Midwestern poetry is to some degree experiential.

*

What are the pitfalls of the Kansas style of writing? As a fifth generation Kansan, I envy my Southern colleagues who tell such good stories at parties and write with such flair. In fact, I am not proposing that Midwestern writing is any standard for the rest of the speakers of English. This simply is my territory, my own dialect, and I have come to accept what I cannot change. I have come to tolerate the condescension of others who mistake the Midwestern reticence for ignorance, and I have learned the necessity of other, more aggressive speech patterns.

One problem is the exclusion of women. In conversation, I have noticed the dominant speakers and storytellers are men, and this carries over into my generation of writers. When I edited two anthologies of Kansas poetry for Cottonwood Press, in 1979 and 1984, I looked especially for women writers, but few were originally from Kansas. Now, ten years later, most of these career women have moved to other states. Lora Reiter of Ottawa and Jane Hoskinson of Lawrence are two who remain. Neither has published a book-length collection. Cynthia Pederson lives in Illinois, but this Topeka woman, author of two books, keeps up ties to Kansas. Patricia Traxler of Salina is a fine writer, and she has a substantial Native American heritage, but she grew up in California. I have served on the board of Woodley Press at Washburn University for ten years, and of the thirty-some books published by that press, two are by women. Cowboy poetry round-ups, which are now popular, seldom include cowgirls. As I have made my way in this literary milieu, I have had no women mentors, no women publishers, and few peers. I have many brothers, but I miss having sisters.

Another issue is the lack of non-white voices in this tradition. There are sizeable Mexican-American, African-American, and now Asian populations in the state. Maybe the somewhat homogenous quality of the writings of Day, Hind, Elliott, and Stafford results from shared gender and race. Other kinds of writers remain unrepresented.

A strength—these Kansas writers have stayed true to their individual directions. They have not made careers of their writing, but rather they pursue it as a way of life. I heard Robert Day speak to this point in a lecture at Washburn University. He discussed the opportunities he had after the publication, with Putnam, of *The Last Cattle Drive,* and what compromises would have been necessary for commercial success. Elliott published with Hanging Loose Press in Brooklyn for years, for a national audience, but he recently refused to move away from Salina when he lost his job as an art professor. His career transpires in his birthplace, and Kansas does not give writers any special rewards. Stafford has

most directly explicated the idea of writing as a meditative discipline rather than career. He says in a PBS interview with Bill Moyers that he does not seek "successful," well-crafted poems. Rather, he writes for the act of discovery, the "adventure" of creating something new. He writes as a means of experiencing human consciousness.

An immigrant into Kansas asked me if the landscape affects the "sense of proportion for the self." How does the scale of sky compared to humans affect the way a plains dweller thinks of herself? Another immigrant from northern Wisconsin, who is used to the cover of forest, remarked on how exposed farm houses are. Anybody can see all sides of the house for miles as they drive by. A person is exposed, too, but can hide through silence. The tendency to conceal the self—translated to poetry as the emphasis on object rather than voice—may be a result of a need to create internal shelter. In the wide open spaces of Kansas farms, it is better to watch strangers first before disclosing personal business.

Understatement is a defense, as well as the ritualized talk about sports and weather. Perhaps surface friendliness is a holdover from frontier days when cooperation was essential for survival on the open range, but danger from unpredictable strangers was always a possibility. Intimacy—whether social or literary—is to be reserved for the most private moments. I do not know any Kansas writers who use the confessional mode.

I am not sure exactly how much anyone can pin down a Kansas, or even a more general Midwestern, style of writing. It would be easy to point to nature as a common subject matter, but many poets write about nature. Henry Taylor makes it clear that people who grow up in different rural settings can write—brilliantly—about nature. I *can*, though, identify shared attitudes that seem to be reflected in the quieter language of writers like Robert Day,

Harley Elliott, Steven Hind, and William Stafford. Some generalities I will suggest: a belief in an infinite mystery, a self-deprecatory attitude (often humorous), and unpretentious language. The culture I grew up in has an anti-intellectual bias, and when I was a child I learned not to flaunt words. Along with swell-headedness, "impudence" was a cardinal sin, so reticence was a means of self-preservation. I learned to listen. Maybe I learned, like Stafford in "Traveling Through the Dark," to listen to the wilderness around me as much as the people. Maybe some day I will be able, like Stafford, to "hear the wilderness listen"—to enter into dialogue with the horizon itself.

At its best, this plains voice can convey faith in the life force—the essence of a heart-felt hymn. But this is not a melody that everyone can hear.

Ed Ruhe's Rooms

What individuals have in Kansas small towns is lots of space and lots of time. Distractions are few, and land is relatively cheap. In 1969, when I was a student, I rented a room in a Victorian house across from the university for $35 a month. It was admittedly seedy, but the location was prime. The downtown rooms a friend of mine, Ed Ruhe, kept for over thirty years in Lawrence were spacious and, I presume, cheap. They made it possible for him to devote his professor's salary to a huge collection of Australian Aborigine bark paintings. From the street no one would guess at the alternative world Ed constructed in his apartment. Looking up from the main street, a person would see only opaque brown windows.

An English professor with a specialty in John Milton, Ed Ruhe also was an adopted member of the Australian aboriginal tribe, the Yirrkala, of Northern Territory. He studied in England, he collected American art works with a certain dark twist, he was a pianist, he collected people. Ultimately, he assembled one of the world's largest collections of Aboriginal bark paintings held in private hands. At his death, a hundred former students and colleagues came together in Lawrence and consoled each other. His family came to ponder the fate of the bark paintings, didjeridoos, spears, and throwing sticks. The final end to Ed's life, and the final revelation of it, came as his rooms were disassembled.

Behind windows of all domiciles, the furniture fits in arrangements that reflect each owner's mind. It seems a law of the physical dimension: domestic objects—tables, rugs, floor lamps, cabinets—eventually migrate to form patterns parallel to human personalities. This is an extension of the law that dogs grow to resemble their owners, or owners come to resemble their dogs. Further, human-tainted rooms take on distinct lives of their own, like the dwellers' own children but in a medium other than flesh. Ed's apartment came to reflect his passion for Australian art forms—and more. In a way, his apartment came a version of Ed Ruhe himself.

The apartment was the upstairs over a downtown movie theater, a rickety fire hazard accessible only by a steep staircases in the front, and alley way stairs in the back. The walls must have been white originally, but decades of smoke and dust had aged them yellow. Ed did not believe in redecorating—it was a waste of time—and he had lived there thirty years. The ceilings were an ancient ivory and twelve feet high, in the style of old office buildings. The apparent living room looked over the downtown street of Lawrence and held his grand piano, a sofa, a sleek coffee table (handmade by Wendell Castle), books, chairs, clutter, and some of the eucalyptus bark paintings.

My favorite bark painting was in the seldom-used living room. It was a striated oblong about five feet by three, brown and ochre with white and black painted designs. I looked at it without comprehension for many years. Only when Ed explained the symbols did the painting take on significance. The arch at the top was a rainbow, and the broken lines at the bottom were prisms. This represented a particular site of Australian ceremonialism, where the dirt has a silicate composition, like glass. Here the men dance with a stomping step, to stir up dust so the sun will refract through the particles like diamonds suspended in the air. Ed used this discussion as a way to impress upon me the sophistication of Aboriginal aesthetics, the refined love of beauty that generated that dance and this painting. He had said in an interview with *Aux Arcs* journal, "There's something like an esthetic sense very appealing and striking among these people: their songs feature matters like that—the sun glinting on the waves, the beautiful design of the sand at Jelangbara, and so on—and it goes into their ceremonies." For me, this painting over the sofa, of Jelangbara, became the focus of the room, a mind-hinge of painted bark. After he died, the last part of his apartment I studied was this painting, trying to burn it into my memory. I knew I would never see it again, at least never again in its proper surrounding.

But the front room was hardly used. It was a parlor, visited only when enough people overflowed the rooms Ed really lived in. The back room, a glassed-in porch with windows on two sides, was the heart of the household. It was at the top of the alley stairs, and when Ed sat at the huge table that filled the room, he could look out over the parking lot that was the site of weekly farmers' markets. Saturday mornings he often bought provisions for his visitors. Across the street he could see an Episcopalian church, which he hated as he hated all vestiges of the Christian religion. But most often he looked not at the outside world, but at the world of words gathered at his table.

The table in Ed's back room held his life. He ate at the end nearest the kitchen, in a space cleared off and covered with a placemat. His typewriter sat at the other end, and around these two focal points were folders, books, letters, manuscripts, typing paper, notecards, postcards, announcements of art openings, museum catalogues—all the detritus of his mind's workings. The walls around the table were lined with bookcases and small tables stacked with more books. In between were bark paintings, three and four deep. Everything he needed, save for a sleeping pallet, was in this room. The table, an altar to the intellect, was like Ed's mind turned inside out—its complexity partitioned into interlocking provinces of order. All his ideas were contained in this shifting topography of paper.

He gathered friends around this table when they came, gave them wine, and occasionally served formal dinners of roast duck and vanilla ice cream with chocolate syrup. He served up extended monologues on the evils of Republicans and European Americans, what they had done to the original peoples of New Zealand and Australia and North America. He pulled out recent acquisitions of art, purchased at a good price—the work of Suzanne Klotz Reilly or David Reismann—or collected at garage sales over the weekend. One tapestry that he found at a garage sale was clearly the design of Joan Miró, he claimed. And here at this table he would discuss his latest research on bark paintings.

On inspired evenings he would pull out the stacks of plastic-covered bark paintings and tell their stories, their relationship to sacred springs and cliffs in Australia, their significance to the clans and their genealogy. Every painting explicated the geography of the Outback. Where European explorers saw only wasteland, the Aborigines had mapped the entire landscape, every slight rise, with complex stories: the paintings were atlases combined with chapters of Genesis. He said, "You see all over Australia the feeling for maps and mapping—in other words, the feeling for their countryside in a bird's-eye view, although they've never flown, seems to be very strong." The paintings indeed were all made like maps, designed to be looked at from above. They were made to rest on the ground during ceremonies, not to hang on walls, so they had to be oriented to eyes looking down on them from all sides.

He would recount his 1960's visit to the Methodist mission in Arnhem Land, where he first met Aboriginal artists, and he referred to some as relatives, like *Bapa*, Father. He would tell the life stories of certain well known artists—Malangi, Wandjuk, Mawalan, and Jawa—and discuss their appearances in movies like *The Right Stuff*. He would rail against their mistreatment at the hands of missionaries, explorers of the past, ranchers, and the Australian government.

On visits when my young sons were present, he interrupted his talk to demonstrate the didjeridoo in the corner, and to play recordings of skilled didjeridoo musicians. This instrument, a tall wooden tube, is designed to create a continuous flow of drones, even when the player takes a breath. He let the boys blow into the instrument, even though it was a museum piece, and when they failed, he demonstrated proper technique.

In the other corner of this room stood a locked specimen cabinet. When he reached a certain level of trust with me, he unlocked some of the drawers and showed me stone spear points and knives. One night when my husband was present, he unlocked one of the lower drawers for him, but asked me to turn away, because these were men's things. I had been around enough Native American doings to respect this, that the sexes are separate, with their separate powers, and American feminism was out of context here. He explained the seriousness of these rules. As recently as the 1950's, Aboriginal women or children who saw sacred objects were speared to death.

In most ways white people were not accountable in the same way as Aborigines. Whites were given even the most secret ceremonial paintings, but they were not explained to them, and after the ceremony, they no longer had power. Ed's aesthetic was not the occult aspects of the paintings, but the residual beauty, as he said of a particular painting, "What we have, for our purposes, is a painting which is weirdly active and beautiful, a product of great skill." I did not press him to see the men's objects of the locked cabinet, and I did not know which paintings were arcane mysteries. I did know the paintings had a magnetic pull. And the cabinet was mysterious like the wardrobes and chests that Gaston Bachelard describes in *The Poetics of Space* as "veritable organs of the secret psychological self."

Ed died suddenly of a heart attack in 1989. He was at the piano in the front room, under the painting of the rainbow. The book on the music stand was turned to an etude, Karl Szymanowski's *Etude,* Opus 4, no. 3, what Evan Tonsing calls a "surprisingly sad, *con dolore* piece." I like to think he was overcome by the passion of the music, though I know death, like childbirth, is not a romantic event. Still, my memories of that room spring to life as I write this: the collection of Edward Gorey books (kept in a plastic garbage sack), the snake effigy on the mantle, the Coptic painting on a goat skin, and people who had been in that room—my sons, English professors, the writer Gerry Shapiro, and another time Robert Day and Fred Whitehead.

When I heard of the death, I phoned the apartment to talk to his nephews, and we asked permission to make a call. I wanted to see the apartment again, since it was not possible to say goodbye to Ed himself.

When we arrived, I was relieved to see that the family had not yet dispersed Ed's belongings, so the scene of his life was still in place. And the nephews had found amazing things. They found Ed had a folder for each person he knew, with letters and publications carefully saved. They had been stacked in the front hall between bookshelves. Hundreds of books remained, and each book—fiction, art, film criticism, theory of postmodernism, British literature, philosophy, and popular culture—had a summary note tucked into the endleaf, with critique.

The bark paintings were everywhere. Altogether they numbered a thousand, including some in storage, and hundreds were in the apartment, unprofessionally preserved except for plastic wrapping. Robert Day describes how they were stacked everywhere—along the walls, under his bed, and "on the piano, and in the closets, and tucked behind the mirrors that hid the Murphy bed." Displays of catalogues and flyers, posted throughout the apartment, commemorated their various showings in Washington D.C., Seattle, New York, Lawrence, and elsewhere.

Other projects were *in media res.* A notebook was found of bark painting reproductions; Ed had been considering these for post cards. Contents of another file revealed he had planned an art book. On the back room table the family also found the extensive manuscript Ed had been reworking, *A Manual of Australian Bark Painting.* The tabletop stacks and files revealed the perfectionism of his scholarship and an orderliness not apparent to casual guests.

Tacked to the wall were flyers for upcoming events, including a photography exhibit of Dzidka Contoski, and English department lectures. Dozens of letters had arrived for Ed, sent by friends before his death, and they were in a new pile by the typewriter.

The cabinet in the corner was now unlocked. Below the drawers of chipped stone tools, his nephew had found a drawer of artifacts wrapped in soft cotton. One was a lozenge of stone, with a mandala-like pattern: pecked lines radiated from the center, which represented the origin of the universe. Ed's nephew explained these lines would put onlookers into a trance during ceremonies. He had been to visit Ed in Australia, and he knew some of the culture. These pieces also were maps, perhaps relating to important springs of water, and further, were representations of the origins of life.

Other rare objects were in the cabinet, including some tools of sorcery. No wonder Ed took care to keep the cabinet locked: he had once said, ". . . I'm a little superstitious, and black magic is known here, see, and I'm just the kind of impressionable person that might come under a curse and wilt away, as people do" (*Aux Arcs* 70). The objects remain un-named, but they came from rituals of Aboriginal witchcraft. As Ed collected the art, he met with many kinds of artists. His motivation was aesthetic, so he avoided tabus or harmful secrets. Still, his love of beauty, as filtered through Aborigine views, put him in contact with certain situations and certain people. He said of an artist he would not name: "Now the art-ist that I'm talking about had evidently been a black magician, because he not only speared people, he also sang them to death, and pointed them to death with pointing bones and incantations" (*Aux Arcs* 71). Ed himself lived to a good age, for he avoided some of these people. Others he could not, and he found out that even his adopted father had practiced witchcraft as a young man. For his own reasons, Ed preserved these objects from a distant desert, and he protected visitors to his apartment as well as he could with a brass lock.

In the bedroom, a room I never entered, the nephew found some of the more sacred paintings, ones that uninitiated men and women should not see. Robert Day recalls Ed would say about the room, "There are spirit objects at rest here that will be dis-turbed by women." The nephew remembered these bark paintings from decades before, during his trip to Australia.

The small dark room had been arranged purpose-fully, unlike the hodge podge of the rest of the apart-ment. The bed was along the wall, neatly made up. The paintings were set in careful order across from the bed. On the dresser, wrapped in cloths, were several stone pieces like the cosmology lozenge in the locked cabinet. Alongside them was an old wallet, wrapped in the same kind of cloth. When the nephew opened it, he found it contained library cards from Allentown, Swarthmore, Columbia, Rutgers, the British Museum, Australia, the University of Kansas, and every other institution Ed had been affiliated with. In sequence, they mapped the course of his scholarship. Library cards appeared to be his sacred objects, the power objects that transformed his world.

There were other caches all over the apartment, in closets and under furniture. There were coin collections, a stamp collection, Native American stone tools (I remembered Ed identifying a flint burin I had found in a Lawrence park) and turquoise jewelry. There was a set of hand-sewn dolls with buttons and human teeth. And there were the bark paintings in every room, the most important objects of the rooms, exuding their particular allure.

I returned several times to see the apartment, and to see his relatives. His imprint on the rooms of the apartment was still distinct. Though I had not seen him often the last years, I now had several dreams about Ed. These were vivid, and in one he urged me to take a bark painting, but I resisted. I could not imagine then, in the dream, how to fit such an anomalous object into my house, and I looked instead for familiar books. In the mornings after these dreams I thought of the Cherokee belief about the days after a person's death being a time of significance, a time when a person's wisdom could be dispersed among the living.

After one of our last visits, a relative told me they all stayed up one night and turned on the audio tapes of Australian clapsticks and didjeridoos. They sat talking and playing Ed's clapsticks along with the recorded music. All night they thought hard of the long journey Ed had to make, so far away from Kansas, to the place he most fully belonged, even more than this apartment filled with books and artifacts.

Finally after two weeks, I dreamed the apartment was bare. I knew Ed Ruhe was in his next abode.

What is Unseen
But Most Potent

One fall afternoon I took a friend to visit Haskell grounds. He was a colleague, a professor at a university in southern Kansas. He had grown up on a Kansas farm, and had an aesthetic for prairie plants. I thought he would enjoy the wildflowers at this season—asters and maximillian sunflowers—and a recent earthworks sculpture—a medicine wheel and thunderbird shaped in grass.

On the way to the Haskell campus, we drove down Massachusetts Street, the main street, named for the abolitionist state that funded settlement of Lawrence. City streets leading to the entrance of Haskell follow the familiar prairie grid the settlers plotted across cuestas and floodplains. From airplanes I have always looked for the interplay of right-angled county roads overlaid on curves of the creek valleys. The city streets, too, follow an angular

progression, for the most part. Aside from unmovable knolls and creeks that skew a few city roads, the city follows the prototype of all small prairie towns. Highways define the city limits, and one offshoot street, out of the traffic pattern, becomes the main street. In the smallest towns, the highway is Main Street. I have visited dozens of small towns, and I know my way around without asking.

But at the entrance to Haskell, this philosophy of civic engineering is left behind. The roads meander around campus, laid out according to another logic. Each road has its own path, and most lead directly to buildings, but the mapping of roads reveals a unique pattern, with some right angles, but also unexpected curves and cul de sacs. Many have relationship to the central commons inhabited by a gazebo. Others take as-the-crow-flies routes to dormitories. In some places a road goes straight up to a blank yard of grass, where a building once existed, but now only the memory remains. Indeed, these ghost buildings still live in the minds of alumni. One of the few books about Haskell is a directory of early buildings. It would have been easy for engineers to lay out a uniform grid for Haskell roads, on the flat floodplain of the Wakarusa River. South campus, in fact, is a continuation of the Baker Wetlands Preserve. But instead, the street layout has developed in an organic fashion, with new parts being added and others left as paths to the past.

As soon as we crossed the boundary between town and Haskell, and as the streets curved as though we were in another dimension, my friend became disoriented. I directed our roundabout path along the western road. This is my favorite view of the wetlands and the glaciated ridge in the distance. The second North American glacier reached to this valley and no further. On fall mornings the frost makes brilliant prisms over the ground, and into the distance the ancient ridge picks up the azure color of

the sky. In summer, dew mutes the bright green of the grass, and morning light is luminous. Though a busy county road cuts the southern edge of campus, it is invisible beyond the wetlands, and behind trees. The earthworks medicine wheel is set in a patch of country that reflects all the seasons like a mirror.

As we drove the meanders to the site of the medicine wheel, my friend continued to talk English professor business, and I pointed out a few landmarks. We turned onto the final gravel road, and he eased the car over sharp gravel and parked on a grassy place behind bushes. As we got out of the car, he hardly glanced around, said nothing about the profusion of wildflowers, and continued to talk about the conference we had just attended and the nature of English departments. I wondered if it had been a good idea to bring him here—maybe we should have gone to a coffee shop downtown.

We walked the mown path toward the edge of the wheel, where a bear paw is cut out of grass, a design about twelve feet across, and suddenly he stopped. I thought he had suddenly taken ill. He grabbed his chest He choked up and his eyes turned red.

I asked if he was okay, but he waved me off. Crickets sounded in the grass around us. Two river gulls flew over.

After a moment he spoke. He said he felt an overpowering sensation of the place that he could not describe.

He stepped back over the invisible boundary and walked forward through it again, and again he felt, in an exact spot, what we could call a force field. English has few words to describe unseen phenomena.

My friend described sensations as though he were in a cathedral, only more concentrated. In the vaulted ceiling of a large church, heaven is embodied by the architectural representation of a firmament. Heaven is a vertical height. Here, in a natural setting, the sense of space extended upward to the sky—and also horizontally, around three hundred sixty degrees. Spirit is connected at the corners of the earth itself, and heavenly bodies of the sky inter-act with the ground in a parallel, not dominating, fashion.

My friend had hardly looked at the grounds as we were driving up and as we walked east to the wetlands site. The entire impact of the design is visible only from an airplane. If a person is expecting colorful totem poles or painted tipis, the medicine wheel and spirit bird are a disappointment. And the eastern Kansas setting is not a dramatic mountainscape nor crashing ocean. What exists at this site is mostly unseen. The physical markers of the four directions and solstice points are just enough to suggest archetypal sky and earth symbols.

My friend was jarred into his experience by subtle cues. The real site of the medicine wheel is within the spirit of the onlooker, and interaction with the guardian spirit—or *genius*—of the place.

The English language continues to contain some old-fashioned words for extrasensory experiences that once were part of literary and theological discourse. *Genius* is one, from the Roman for "tutelary and controlling spirit connected with a place." This word appears in English in *Romance of the Rose* (1390), works of Drayton, Shakespeare, and Dryden. Ghost, goblin, werewolf, haunted, weird, druid, conjurer, leprechaun, magic, fairy, angel, cherubim, seraphim, and other words have become marginalized terms. I am not naive enough to propose that if a word exists, it must be a proven reality. Jack Weatherford calls this "naïve realism," an anthropological term that means people's language exactly matches up to the world. Yet these words once had significance, and if imaginary, they do translate across many cultures. I cannot think of a culture that does not have some kind of word for ghosts. Perhaps that suggests many people have experiences where that word has authentic significance. Or perhaps the human imagination works in a similar manner.

But anyone who has seen a woodblock print of a ghost rendered by the Japanese artist Yoshitoshi must have some level of belief in the vibrancy of the human spirit after death. Anyone who has seen

Bernini's "The Ecstasy of St. Theresa" must also see the reality of religious feeling.

The Bible contains numerous references to prophetic dreams, visions, miracles, and spirits, but since the nineteenth century these have been omitted from the discourse of most churches, except in a historic sense. They are not expected to be the experience of contemporary worshippers, in most denominations. The doctrine of most churches now joins together faith with good works. This is a practical, not a mystical age.

But what is unseen does have reality—sometimes the most important reality. Take love. I found out about this when writing a series of alchemical love poems,

> . . .*some fire hung*
> *between my throat and belly*
> *to burn and pull me outside,*
> *to a lover and to children:*
> *the part of me most unseen*
> *and most potent*

Denise Low

Mother love, an intangible quality, has a parallel in the smallest plant parts—seeds, corms, and bulbs:

The one-chambered tulip bulb
too becomes an ember underground,
a charged lump within pieces of dirt.

Underground, and within the human body, the most powerful forces express themselves. They have ab-solute reality, yet they are invisible. At the medicine wheel, what is most important is that which is not visible. The symbols and the land ignite within human imagination of them. The medicine wheel is a grass, four stones, and four fire pits. Yet this tracing of patterns in grass has the power to stop a man in his tracks.

Haskell Earthworks Medicine Wheel

A hawk floats overhead, not moving its outspread wings. Below in the grass, mice startle when they see the shadow. The hawk sees any movement of gray fur through green blades, and also at that height it sees the thunderbird and medicine wheel designs cut into the field. These earth art designs at Haskell Indian Nations University are on the scale of prehistoric structures like the Serpent Mound or the Big Horn Medicine Wheel—over four acres in all. Most mornings the hawk can be seen gliding over this territory, an unmoving outline.

Cut grass outlines the medicine wheel circle within a pasture of free-growing wildflowers and brome grass, and four mowed paths divide the circle into fourths. The paths align with magnetic north, and also sunrise and sunset. Cairns stand at pathway entrances. The inner circle, a clear space about twenty yards across, has a stone-lined fire pit at the exact center. Stones also outline fire pits just outside the circle to the North and South, next to raised grass designs of deer tracks.

Leslie Evans, a painter and sculptor of Potawatomi descent, and Stan Herd, an earthworks artist, created the Earthworks Medicine Wheel as a way of joining past and present Native American traditions. The human symbols are completed by nature itself—the foraging hawk, the sky, and the earth.

*

When Stan Herd presented the Earthworks Medicine Wheel to the Haskell faculty and staff, with Evans, he described growing up as a non-Indian on a Kansas farm. He said that even as a child he al-

ways had a sense of living in someone else's country. The indigenous people who lived there for millennia left more than place names with the land. He felt a continuing presence of history, perhaps a presence articulated by Seattle, or Sealth, in his speech to the governor of Washington territory in 1854. Henry Smith translated his words:

> . . . these shores will swarm with the invisible dead of my tribe, and when your children's children think themselves alone in the field, the store, the shop, upon the highway, or in the silence of the pathless woods, they will not be alone.

Events wed themselves to a place, and these histories resonate there, in hauntings. Stan Herd felt the histories of his parents' fields, and those feelings stayed with him all his life.

*

The dramatic scale of open Kansas plains affects all peoples in some way. Some travelers through the plains get a form of agoraphobia and lose all sense of direction. Or sometimes the experience of such space is exhilarating to the human imagination. Gaston Bachelard wrote about open seascapes and landscapes, and their importance to people. He believed concepts like "immensity" depend on natural settings and become internalized— "immensity is a philosophical category of daydream." Features of the land blend into consciousness of people living within it. Artworks of a large scale like medicine wheels are compatible with people who see open skies every day.

My great-great-grandfather's writings show a change after he moved west from Kentucky to Kansas in 1877. William A. Dotson added grander metaphors to his column for the national *Methodist Monthly*, "There is power in the electric bolt as it rides the crest of the clouds and flings coruscations through the fields of immensity. . . ." Lightning bolts and immense space had new meaning to him after thunderstorms of the magnitude seen in Kansas, and his imagination stretched to include new images for the words "power" and "immensity."

Land interacts with the workings of mind, and textures of a landscape become affixed to its sojourners. Like rocks, layers of histories also settle in place, in a sedimentary process. Sometimes histories of people take tangible form, in symbolic structures of stone and earth.

*

Evans designed the Haskell project to blend Great Plains medicine wheels with the tradition of Mississippi Valley effigy mounds. He further incorporated motifs of the Southwest Pueblo, and those of the northern woodlands. And many tribes have the tradition of a central fire pit.

The bear paw part of the Earthworks Medicine Wheel came into existence after the wheel and bird, on September 12, 1992. Wind blew from cloud-filled sky, but no rain fell. Small branched sunflowers, Maximilian sunflowers, were in full bloom around the horizon.

West of the circle Leslie Evans and Stan Herd measured out a grid scaled to the original drawing. They marked intervals of green grass with red flags, and Herd shaped the grass with a weed cutter, free-hand, stopping occasionally to gauge the drawing to the ground pattern. The rounded paw emerged, and then four claws turned into the dirt. The artists will bring in stones or earth to flesh out the open hand of this power animal. In northern traditions around the Arctic Circle, the bear represents shamanism.

*

The site for the Medicine Wheel lies south of the Haskell campus buildings, in wetlands of the Wakarusa Valley. The southernmost glaciation terminated within sight of Haskell, and carved out the wide valley. The tract of land—over 200 acres—remains undeveloped, a peninsula of wild growth surrounded by the city of Lawrence. The land often flooded before construction of Clinton Dam, and the sound of bullfrogs comes from small creeks leading to the Wakarusa River.

Over a hundred years ago the land was part of Haskell Institute—a Bureau of Indian Affairs school for Native American children. This was part of the government programme to erradicate Native cultures. A cemetery on the southeastern corner of the main campus commemorates the children who did not survive cold winters and poor food of the first years, 1884 to the early 1900s. Fragments of worked iron and square nails turn up near the old stable, in the yard once used for shoeing horses. Little else remains of this Haskell legacy.

*

Many of the first children were of the Ponca nation. Ponca people held powwows as early as 1876, and their families carried the tradition of these intertribal meetings to Haskell during the early part of the century. They camped in the pastures, drummed and sang traditional music, and danced. Augustus McDonald, a Ponca, won first place in the traditional, war, and fancy dancing categories at the Haskell powwow in 1926. This was when fancy dancing was new, and Frank McDonald of the Haskell staff described the dress of the fancy dancers, with bells and "bright metal hoops," from the hoop dance. He described the dance steps— "the symmetrical motion of moving their feet faster than a sprinter's start."

The legendary 1926 powwow occurred to mark the dedication of the Haskell stadium and arch. During the four-day celebration, newspapers estimated over one hundred thousand people came from all over the country, and tents covered the grounds of the medicine wheel site. Haskell built an "Indian Village" for the occasion, twenty city blocks with street lights and water to each block. Seventy tribal groups camped there. Louis Bighorse acquired four buffalo and thirteen steers, and he and his workers spent ten days preparing barbecue. Among the notable persons were Two Guns White

Calf, whose profile is on the buffalo nickel, and United States Senator Charles Curtis, of the Kaw tribe. Old warriors were still alive then, and renewed acquaintances. The Blackfeet chief Bull Calf said he met an old foe at the Haskell stadium dedication, "White Buffalo acts like he doesn't know me, but he does all right. I shot him in the ear in a war many years ago." Other tribal leaders were Chief Bacon Rind, Fred Lookout, John Quapaw, White Buffalo, and White Cloud.

*

The school became a junior college in 1970. The road to the south part of campus no longer led to an Indian Village or cow pastures and gardens. Instead, it became infamous as Forty-Nine Road, named for the late night parties after powwows. Veterans of those days still tell stories about fights, quick courtships, songs, and other experiences on this party road.

Today the dirt road leads past a cross country runners course, past the campus dump heap, and past utility wires. Nothing tangible remains of floods, powwows, young students, or the night wind that blew past them.

The Medicine Wheel site is just east of Forty-Nine Road, up a slight rise. Space gathers itself around a whorl of grass and tilts into sunrise sky.

*

The words "medicine wheel" and "earthworks" have their own history as translations of Native American experience. "Medicine" first came into English in the term "medicine man" or "medicine woman," the healers of a Native American tribe. "Medicine" might be translated today as "healing" or "power," or both these ideas at once, the creation of psychic and physical wholeness. And "wheel" might be reworded as "hoop." Laguna and Sioux author Paula Gunn Allen titled a book *The Sacred Hoop,* and maybe this would be a more accurate term. But the words "medicine wheel" have found their place in American English.

Traditional medicine wheels are huge spoked circles outlined by stones. They date at least as far back as 4500 years ago, the time of Stonehenge and Egyptian pyramids of the Old Kingdom. Stone cairns center them, and they reflect the sky in their arrangements—sunrise and sunset points, winter and summer solstices, and various stars. Most of the fifty known medicine wheels are in Canada, on the eastern barrens of the Canadian Rockies.

Astronomy is apparent in the design of the Big Horn Medicine Wheel, between Sheridan and Lovell, Wyoming. Summer solstice was marked to correspond to star alignments from 200 to 700 years ago. Three stars—Aldebaran, Rigel, and Sirius—rose at dawn during those summer months, each a month apart. Three cairns mark the paths of those stars, as the summer calendar of prehistoric nomads who traveled North every summer to live off the land. The Big Horn Wheel design also resembles one of the Cheyenne Sun Dance Lodge layouts, with twenty-eight radiating rafters and an altar at the west.

The oldest medicine wheel, in Alberta, dates to 4500 years ago. Its central cairn includes fifty tons of stones and shows evidence of use for at least 4000 years, but vandals have destroyed its outline. Its original alignments are blurred.

Another ancient wheel, made of moss-covered stones, lies in Rocky Mountain National Park near a Ute trail over the Continental Divide. One of its spokes lines up with the summer solstice.

Some medicine wheels decorate the solstice spoke with a small sun symbol, an outline of smaller stones, so its purpose is clear.

*

Earthworks also remain from traditional Native American cultures. They are shapes made of mounded dirt, from a few inches to sixty-five feet in height. They vary: effigy mounds appear in Wisconsin, Michigan, and Iowa—often birds, snakes and bears; dome-shaped burial mounds and flat-topped pyramids in the Ohio Valley; and temple mounds in southern states like Mayan pyramids.

Native Americans of the eastern part of the country also made earthworks embankments from five to thirty feet high, as walls for defense and refuge during floods. Where European and Central American peoples tended to use stone, early Midwesterners used the earth itself.

*

Earthworks mounds—and medicine wheels—are measuring tools for the sky. People built these large-scale designs in relationship to movements of sun, moon, and stars. Besides the importance of sky cycles to planting and harvest, timing is also important for following the movements of animals for hunting. All matter, even the substance of stars, resurrects itself into various patterns, and then disintegrates to re-form, or as Loren Eiseley phrased this, "Form is an illusion of time." Each day people change earth's minerals, or stardust, into flesh; they are not so distant from the sky after all.

Some of the earthworks mounds of the Mississippi and Ohio Valleys echo star constellations. Cluster mounds in Hamilton County, Ohio, correspond to the Pleides. They also form a bear paw. The Marching Bear Group of mounds in McGregor, Iowa, follows the pattern of the Big Dipper, and solstice alignments appear at the Cahokia mounds near St. Louis.

The last temple mound tribe, the Natchez, had a leader named the "Sun" of his tribe, and other aspects of astronomy may have been part of their culture as described by French traders.

*

One of the oldest plains groups illustrates how crucial sky patterns were to early people. In Nebraska the Skidi Pawnee people laid out over a dozen villages in the pattern of the four directions and the

North Star, evening and morning stars, and others. They also set their earth lodge posts in the same pattern, so houses and the arrangement of villages harmonized with patron stars.

*

The Haskell Earthworks Medicine Wheel design emphasizes close relationship between people and the sky. The circle opens at the sunrise point of the spring and fall equinoxes, and the western point where the sun falls below the horizon. The center of the circle is a hearth for fire, the element of stars. And fire is the breath of the Earth, which is molten at its core.

The Medicine Wheel has already existed for years, within the patterns of moon, stars, wild flowers, animals, and all peoples who have shared Haskell prairieland. It existed in the imaginations of the early Pawnee and the builders of Stonehenge.

Now a contemporary arrangement of grass, mounds, rocks, trees, and fire hearth come together within a new spectrum of time. The new medicine wheel helps people remember interlocking patterns of life, as Earth carries all histories through spires of sky.

*

One hot afternoon I walked Forty-Nine Road to the cleared space of the Medicine Wheel. Wind carried the pungent smell of cut grass. A curve appeared in the expanse of land, to the east, and at the southern horizon was a line of trees following drainage patterns worn into earth many seasons ago. A distant bank of sunflowers made a yellow shadow at the western edge of sky.

Since the land around the Medicine Wheel no longer is planted in brome hay, native plants reestablish themselves. Asters, spiky golden rod, sunflowers, yarrow, white snakeroot, hedge glorybind, red clover, and milkweed all bloomed this day in colorful resurgence: late summer is peak flowering season of the prairie. Grasses, too, grew in unexpected variety—little bluestem, turkey foot bluestem, sedges, and foxtail.

I followed a section of the newly cut Medicine Wheel pattern and felt a larger sense of scale—an immensity of space and of time. I felt as I stood at the center that this was the exact starting point of the Earth. Trees followed the far rise of land to the east, and fields stretched forever into south, west, and north. Sky was a brilliant blue heaven.

*

Black Elk told John Neihardt, "Everything an Indian does is in a circle, and that is because the Power of the World always works in circles. . . . The sky is round, and I have heard that the earth is round like a ball, and so are the stars." The Earthworks Medicine Wheel echoes natural patterns of a bird's egg or a tree trunk.

Hawks, river gulls, grass snakes, crickets, grasshoppers, butterflies, black and red ants, bees, and rabbits all share Haskell land. It embodies circular motions of moon, sun, and stars. Four paths within the circle represent the four stages of human life; winds of the four directions; the elements earth, air, fire, and water; wisdom of the four grandfathers of creation; and four seasons. Invocation of the four directions anchors a sense of place—Native American spirituality is bound to specific localities of the Earth, exact sites.

Lightning

One night we drove through a stormfront into a landscape of sleety rain and fireball lightning on every side of the road. The clouds were so low the car seemed to move through sky rather than ground. We expected the fragile metal around us to explode.

For fifty miles we experienced unreal water and fire: rain fell in slabs, and lightning went off like land mines all around the car. For hours wind moved against earth in a frenzied dialogue.

We witnessed this and lived.

*

Usually a storm follows a regular sequence. First the thunderhead looms higher until it dominates the sky. At last it blocks out the sun. The hush of quiet air seems to hang forever as wind direction shifts. Then a quickening of cold wind, faint thunder, and spatters of rain build to a torrent as the front passes through, with lightning and thunder firing at once. Finally it slacks off, and a steady driving rain settles in for the night.

This last rain is the best sleeping song outside the womb.

*

Lightning is a complete language. The fundamental grammar is simple — bolts touch ground or do not; strikes split clouds singly or in branching veins of sparks.

Horizontal lightning flickers from cloud to cloud, aloft, brightening cloud banks from within. From a distance, they are silent. But lightning aimed at earth in jagged perpendiculars are accompanied by violent noise.

Denise Low

Some rainstorms move quickly, with simple dynamics of distance and arrival—pianissimo and fortissimo. Some ramble for days around one spot, circling west, east, northeast, west.

Surprise is crucial. Intervals between thunder jolts are irregular, syncopated against regular pulses of bloodflow.

The quiet moment afterwards deepens into a pause like the hushed moment after a storyteller ends a thought.

Spring Firing of the Bluestem Prairie

Black Elk. *The Sacred Pipe: Black Elk's Account of the Seven Rites of the Oglala Sioux.* Ed. Joseph Epes Brown. Baltimore: Penguin, 1971. 5-7.

Heat-Moon, William Least. *PrairyErth: A Deep Map.* Boston: Houghton Mifflin, 1991. 76-80.

Hoy, James. "Controlled Pasture Burning in the Folklife of the Kansas Flint Hills." *Great Plains Q* 9 (Fall 1989): 231-8.

—. "Pasture Burning in the Flint Hills." *Kansas School Naturalist* 39.2 (March 1993): 3-7.

—. "To Start a Fire." *Kansas School Naturalist* 39.2 (March 1993): 7-11.

Launchbaugh, J.L. "Effect of Fire on Shortgrass and Mixed Prairie Species." *Proceedings: Annual Tall Timbers Fire Ecology Conference.* 8-9 June 1972. Lubbock: Koko Palace Auditorium, 1973.

Pyne, Stephen J. *Fire in America: A Cultural History of Wildland and Rural Fire.* Princeton: Princeton UP 1982.

Sauer, Carl O. *Selected Essays 1963-1975.* Berkeley: Turtle Island Foundation, 1981.

Smith, E.F. and C.E. Owensby. "Effects of Fire on True Prairie Grasslands." *Proceedings: Annual Tall Timbers Fire Ecology Conference.* 8-9 June 1972. Lubbock: Koko Palace Auditorium ,1972.

Stevens, William K. "Restoring an Ancient Landscape: An Innovative Plan for the Midwest." *New York Times* 2 March 1993: B5+.

Mourning Wreaths of Human Hair

Black Elk. *The Sacred Pipe: Black Elk's Account of the Seven Rites of the Oglala Sioux.* Ed. Joseph Epes Brown. Baltimore: Penguin, 1971. 12-3.

Fanny Appleton Longfellow. *Mrs. Longfellow: Selected Letters and Journal.* Ed. Edward Wagenknecht. New York: Longmans, Green, 1956. 142.

Alice Marriott and Carol K. Rachlin, eds. *Plains Indian Mythology.* New York: Mentor, 1975.

Nancy Smith. "Family Album Features Hair, Not Photographs." *Lawrence Journal World* 10 Jan. 1992.

Carrie Adel Strittmatter. Unpublished journal. 1958.

Glenway Wescott. *The Grandmothers.* New York: Atheneum, 1955. 10-11.

At Home on the Range: Kansas Vernacular in Literature

Atkins, Douglas G. *Estranging the Familiar: Toward a Revitalized Critical Writing.* Athens: U of Georgia P, 1992.

Day, Robert. *The Last Cattle Drive.* Rpt. Lawrence: UP of Kansas, 1983.

—. *Speaking French in Kansas and Other Stories.* Lawrence: Cottonwood, 1989.

Dekker, Michael. "Russian Students Find KU a Limiting Experience." *Lawrence Journal-World* 7 May 1994: B-1.

Elliott, Harley. *Darkness at Each Elbow.* Brooklyn: Hanging Loose, 1981.

—. *The Secret Lover Poems*. Tempe: Emerald City, 1977.

Hall, Edward T. *The Hidden Dimension*. New York: Anchor, 1969.

Henson, Lance. *Selected Poems 1970-1983*. Greenfield Center, New York: Greenfield Review, 1985.

—. Poetry Reading. Haskell Indian Nations University, 1985.

Hind, Steven. *That Trick of Silence.* Topeka: Washburn University Center for Kansas Studies, 1990.

Hoy, James. "Prairie Fires: Pasture Burning in the Flint Hills." *The Kansas School Naturalist* 39.2 (March 1993): 3-7.

Jackson, Wes. *Altars of Unhewn Stone: Science and the Earth*. San Francisco: North Point P, 1987.

Kitchen, Judith. *Understanding William Stafford.* Columbia: U of South Carolina P, 1989.

Leap, William. *American Indian English*. Salt Lake City: U of Utah P, 1994.

Low, Denise, ed. *Kansas Poems of William Stafford*. Topeka: Woodley, 1990.

—. Interview. *Cottonwood* 48 (Fall 1993): 72-3.

Meats, Stephen. *Looking for the Pale Eagle*. Topeka: Woodley, 1993.

Olson, Charles. *Selected Writings of Charles Olson*. Ed. Robert Creeley. New York: New Directions, 1966.

About the Photographer

GEORGE KREN'S work has been published in the *Kansas Art Reader* and *Kansas Quarterly*. The cover of the book *Landscapes* by Robert Sudlow features George's photo of the artist. His work has appeared in a host of invitational shows throughout the Midwest, among them "Not Just Another Pretty Face," held at the Wichita Art Museum (1987), and juried shows, including the Five State Photography Exhibition in Hayes, Kansas (1986 and 1990).

George's slide program "Kansans on Kansas: An Inquiry into Values" was sponsored by the Kansas Committee for the Humanities. His photographs of Kansas artists make up part of the permanent collection of the Spencer Museum and Kansas Collection, University of Kansas Libraries. His photograph of Elizabeth Layton is in the permanent collection of the Lawrence Art Center.

George Kren is a professor of History at Kansas State University and lives in Manhattan.

About the Author

DENISE LOW's books of poems include *Vanishing Point, Selective Amnesia, Starwater, Spring Geese, Dragon Kite* and *Tulip Elegies: An Alchemy of Writing.* She edited *Kansas Poems of William Stafford* and *Confluence: Contemporary Kansas Poets.*

Her work has been anthologized in publications from Harper & Row, Random House, Helicon Nine, Vintage '45 Press, Windflower Press and Monitor Book Co.

She has won awards and fellowships from the Kansas Arts Commission, the Roberts Foundation, National Endowment for the Arts, the Newberry Library, Lichtor Poetry Prizes, Academy of American Poets, Pami Jurassi Bush Awards and Seaton Awards.

Denise Low is a fifth generation Kansan. She teaches Creative Writing at Haskell Indian Nations University in Lawrence, Kansas.